*"As newborn babes,
desire the sincere milk of the word,
that ye may grow thereby."
(1 Peter 2:2 KJV)*

THE FAMILY BIBLE COMPANION

Janice Y. Cook & Kathy J. Comina

INTERVARSITY PRESS
DOWNERS GROVE, ILLINOIS 60515

InterVarsity Press is the book-publishing division of InterVarsity Christian Fellowship, a student movement active on campus at hundreds of universities, colleges and schools of nursing in the United States of America, and a member movement of the International Fellowship of Evangelical Students. For information about local and regional activities, write Public Relations Dept., InterVarsity Christian Fellowship, 6400 Schroeder Rd., P.O. Box 7895, Madison, WI 53707-7895.

Cover illustration: Donna Nelson

ISBN 0-8308-1173-7

Printed in the United States of America ∞

Library of Congress Cataloging-in-Publication Data

Cook, Janice Y.
    The family Bible companion/by Janice Y. Cook & Kathy J. Comina.
      p.   cm.
    ISBN 0-8308-1173-7
    1. Bible—Study.   I. Comina, Kathy J.   II. Title.
  BS600.2.C65   1991
220'.07—dc20   91-21908
                                                CIP

15	14	13	12	11	10	9	8	7	6	5	4	3
03	02	01	00	99	98	97	96	95	94			

To our children:
Sarah and Matthew
Zane and Christine
for lending us your minds,
hearts and perspectives.

To families everywhere,
often seen as weary travelers
in a busy world,
take courage as you seek closeness
with one another and with God.

week	book	page	date started	date finished

Welcome to Family Bible Study

The joy you encountered with your first scoop of double fudge marshmallow ripple cannot be compared to the anticipation for the next scoop. Your appetite cannot be whetted until you make a commitment to taking that very first taste.

If you've ever attempted to encourage small children to try something new and different, you know that it can be very difficult, especially if it wasn't their desire in the first place. However, their desire will be increased and nurtured only after that first experience.

The traditions we create with our families become a rich source of learning, development and exploration for all members. When family time is centered around Bible study, with participation and communication as its base, children and parents alike are given the opportunity to witness the awakening spirituality in one another.

There is a place within each of us that yearns for a closeness to and a knowledge of God. Within that place is born desire which is kept alive by the nurture of the Holy Spirit. This desire grows and is fed out of our commitment to accept, acknowledge and experience his presence and action. One of the important facets of this relationship is studying and understanding the Bible.

It is our hope that *The Family Bible Companion* will offer a viable way for you and your family to cultivate a habit of regular Bible study.

In his loving hands,
Janice and Kathy

How to Use
The Family Bible Companion

Our goal is to introduce people of all ages to the rewards of daily Bible study. Our desire is to create a generation of biblically literate adults and children, engaging them in an ongoing quest for knowledge that can lead to a deepening relationship with God. In addition, we hope this study will be an enabling tool in placing the guidance, leadership and responsibility for the spiritual awakening and development of children in the loving hands of family.

What Is This Book?
The Family Bible Companion is:

1. A home Bible study program designed for people of all ages.

2. A fifty-two-week overview of the Bible.

3. Designed so that study can be done six days a week in as little as ten minutes each day.

4. A passage of Scripture followed by two questions. The first question focuses on the content of the passage and encourages

your family to dig into the Scriptures. The second question is meant to stimulate a dialog between family members which helps to apply and relate Scripture to their everyday life.

5. Designed to accommodate a broad spectrum of ages. Because the questions are very general, it is impossible to be age-appropriate for everyone. We encourage you to be creative in adapting this program for your children.

How Do I Lead My Family in the Studies?

1. Try to find a regular time each day and allow at least ten minutes to work on your Bible study. Commit your family to that time and make every effort to keep that commitment. Recognize that in today's family there is a need for flexibility. Some suggestions on creatively using the Bible study are:

☐ As the family gathers for a meal, read the Bible passage and use the questions to stimulate meaningful mealtime dialog.

☐ Traveling with your family, whether a short distance to school and work or longer trips, can be a great opportunity for a family to do the studies. Ahead of time, have a family member record the Bible passage and questions on a cassette to use in the car.

☐ For a special focus time with one child, use the Bible study with your children individually. This can also be done when time does not permit the entire family to be together.

2. To record your family's progress, date each week of completed study on the chart at the front of the book. You might also want to include the names of family members who participate. Family members will be encouraged by these names and dates.

3. Use a translation that is easy for everyone to understand. The *New International Version, Today's English Version,* and the *New Revised Standard Version* are all recommended.

4. Familiarize yourself with the set-up of the book, including the Old Testament Rulers and Prophets chart on page 47 and the glossary which begins on page 147. Refer to these during your studies. In many of the studies and in the first study for each book, you'll find transitional statements in smaller type which help you weave together the studies and the portions of Scripture which aren't read. These short introductions and conclusions will help you answer questions from your family. You may want to read them aloud or paraphrase them as they occur or just refer to them as questions arise.

5. Memory work can be a source of encouragement and comfort. A weekly memory verse is provided for you to use with your family. Some suggestions on how to learn the verses are:

☐ Keep the memory verse posted on your refrigerator at the beginning of the week.

☐ Write the memory verse on an index card, and keep it in the car to learn during travel time.

☐ Encourage your family members to learn the verse through an activity. One way to do this is with a memory puzzle. Write the memory verse in large letters on a sheet of paper. Cut the paper into puzzle pieces, mix them up and time your family to see how fast they can put it back together.

☐ Keep a daily record of who can say the verse by memory.

☐ The memory verse can be used to enrich your family devotion and prayer life. Use it at mealtime, bedtime and any time you want to.

6. Efforts should be made to give all family members with reading ability the opportunity to read aloud from the Bible. This can be done by sentences, verses or whole passages. Try not to be too concerned with exact pronunciation, but rather focus on the content of the Scriptures.

7. Sharing and modeling are important aspects of the Christian life and equally important using *The Family Bible Companion*. Children and parents alike will be enriched by the open participation of all family members. Sometimes it is helpful for the parents to begin the sharing process. Honest communication can lead to fantastic discussions!

8. For the most effective results, it is best to follow the days of the week in chronological order. For example, if your family completes Day One on Monday and is unable to continue until Friday, pick up with Day Two.

9. Close your studies in prayer. Recognize that each person has a unique style of communicating with God and must develop his or her confidence in praying aloud. Through the course of the study, encourage different family members to lead in prayer. When time permits, group prayer is an enriching experience. Allow each family member an opportunity to pray, respecting those who would rather be silent.

10. There are special activities throughout the book that are meant to strengthen the point of that week's Scripture focus. The instructions are general, allowing you to use these ideas as you wish. Take advantage of these to enhance family learning and fellowship.

Is This Appropriate for My Child's Age?

The Family Bible Companion can be an effective tool for home Bible study for all ages when used creatively and with some understanding of the developmental personality of your children. We hope the following information will aid you in that understanding.

Preschool-Age Children

Preschoolers are very open to hearing the Word of God. At about three years old children are beginning to understand that Jesus loves them, and they experience times of spontaneous wonder. They are also able to recognize that the Bible is different from other books. These children are ready to respond when you talk with them.

1. Passages for preschool children have been shortened in some cases to be more appropriate for a preschooler's attention span.

2. It would be helpful if you do the Bible study yourself first, and then present it to your family. You may find that you need to shorten the reading selection.

3. If there are questions that appear too difficult for your children, try and simplify them. However, it is important to remember that an honest and thoughtful response by parents can lead to a valuable learning and modeling experience.

4. At this age children interpret things very literally. For example, my three-year-old daughter was upset when she heard that Jesus lived in her heart because she was afraid of a person living inside her body. Avoid symbolic language and try to keep discussions in concrete terms.

5. Your children may have difficulty understanding some acts of God, especially those that include punishment. For example, because Jeremiah's prophecies of doom and exile are not immediately countered with God's constant and abiding faith and care, your children may see God's actions as being mean or monstrous. It would be wise to present this example within the context of a loving parent dealing with a recalcitrant child. Help your children understand, within their own context, the "consequences" of disobedience.

Kindergarten-Age Children

Kindergartners are beginning to see the difference between right and wrong. They are open to learn about God and have a simple trust in him. At this time, they can experience real worship. Because they are very literally minded, they can accept what they are told about God.

Remember that at this age children have a limited vocabulary and a short attention span. They can memorize, but they forget quickly.

Primary-Age Children (6-8 years)
Primary school children are open to learning about God and accept almost everything they are told or exposed to about him. Even though they are not able to think logically about God or express their feelings, they are able to talk with God easily if encouraged by family. They are beginning to read and can recognize familiar Bible verses.

The second question each day, which focuses on personal application, will have particular significance at this age because children live in the now and have little sense of time.

Middler-Age Children (8-10 years)
Middler children are beginning to formulate questions about Christianity. They enjoy participating in worship and are familiar with Bible verses. The children are open to learn about God and have developed a sense of right and wrong in attitudes and actions toward others. At this age, it is important to strengthen their self-image as children of God who are loved by God.

This can be an exciting time for your family to study together because middler-age children would rather participate than watch. They have also developed an ability to reason, discuss and are very curious, asking many questions. Additionally, children at this age have a lengthening attention span and good memories.

Junior-Age Children (10-11 years)

Junior-aged children question and evaluate different points of view in search of their own convictions and are growing in faith as their concepts mature. They can sense the relevance of the Bible to their decisions and behavior. At this age they understand historical relationships and their significance for the Christian faith. They have developed their ability to think, reason and solve problems and the ability to express religious thoughts.

Junior-High Youth (12-14 years)

Junior-high youth are able to discover the relevance of the Bible to their decisions. They question everything, challenge adult thinking and have developed the ability to think, reason and ask questions. While they may have doubts, they search for, question and evaluate their own convictions and experiences.

High School (15-17 years)

Adolescence is a time of transition and change. One of the greatest areas of change from preadolescence to adulthood is in the area of cognitive intellectual development. They are moving from concrete thinking to a more abstract way of thinking.

During this stage, adolescents tend to be curious, adventuresome, open to new ideas, inventive and often a bit idealistic. This new stage of intellectual development has important implications in faith development as these young people are beginning to focus on questions like "Who am I?" "How can I know?" and "What is life all about?" In the adolescent years discussion becomes the key to good learning. This is an important time to ask rather than to tell.

At this time of life teenagers are also developing autonomy.

Because this is a very private time of life, your children may not like the idea of family study—especially if you have not read the Bible together before. They may be willing to be open with their peers, but not with parents. Encourage them to do personal Bible study or to study with other peers even if they don't want to study as a family.

Steps for Daily Study

1. Pray that God may bless your understanding of his Word. Encourage taking turns praying.

2. Read the Bible passage aloud. Parents, and children that are readers, share in the reading responsibilities.

3. Read question one aloud. This will help give you a focus for that passage. Have your children answer the questions first to see what their understanding is. This will help give insight to your children's perspective and clarify any misconceptions. Parents, be sure to answer questions also.

4. Use question two to stimulate more personal dialog and discussion.

5. Use the space in the table of contents to keep a record of the date you complete each study.

6. If you want to use the key memory verse for the week, study it during your time together each day or encourage family members to work on it separately and then set aside a day each week to take turns saying it.

7. Close with prayer.

Books and Divisions of the Bible

Old Testament

1. Books of the Law (the Pentateuch)
These books tell about the origins of the Jewish people and culture.

Genesis	Numbers
Exodus	Deuteronomy
Leviticus	

2. History Books
The history of the Israelites continues as they move into the land of Canaan and establish a kingdom that lasts almost 500 years.

Joshua	2 Samuel	2 Chronicles
Judges	1 Kings	Eza
Ruth	2 Kings	Nehemiah
1 Samuel	1 Chronicles	Esther

3. Books of Poetry
The books of poetry concentrate on questions concerning God, love, life and pain.

Job	Ecclesiastes
Psalms	Song of Songs
Proverbs	

4. The Prophets
When kings ruled Israel and Judah, God spoke through prophets. The primary goal of these prophets was to call God's people back to him.

Isaiah	Joel	Habakkuk
Jeremiah	Amos	Zephaniah
Lamentations	Obadiah	Haggai
Ezekiel	Jonah	Zechariah
Daniel	Micah	Malachi
Hosea	Nahum	

New Testament
5. The Gospels
Gospel means "good news." These four books are accounts of the life of Jesus and the good news he brought to earth.

Matthew	Luke
Mark	John

6. Church History
This book is the account of the first days of the Christian church and what happened to Jesus' followers after he left them.

Acts

7. Letters
Many of these were written by the apostle Paul, who led the advance of Christianity to non-Jewish people. Other followers of Christ also set down their beliefs and messages to help nourish the young church.

Romans	2 Thessalonians	2 Peter
1 Corinthians	1 Timothy	1 John
2 Corinthians	2 Timothy	2 John
Galatians	Titus	3 John
Ephesians	Philemon	Jude
Philippians	Hebrews	Revelation
Colossians	James	
1 Thessalonians	1 Peter	

Part 1
Books of the Law

Genesis
Exodus
Leviticus
Numbers
Deuteronomy

Week 1

Key Memory Verse: "God saw all that he had made, and it was very good"
(Genesis 1:31).

Day 1. Story of Creation. Genesis 1:1-24

Genesis, meaning "beginning," covers the times from the creation (that is, the beginning of history) to the history of God's first Israelite leaders. This book gives us the origins of the Jewish people and culture.

1. When we first meet God in the Bible, what do we see him doing?

2. God describes his creation as "good." List three "good" things about yourself.

Day 2. Ruling Creation. Genesis 1:25-31.

1. Name some of the things that God made for humans to rule over.

2. Ruling over means "taking care of." What are some ways we can take care of the earth and all living things on it?

Day 3. Story of Adam and Eve. Genesis 2.

1. Who did God create next?

2. God did not want his creation to be lonely. Have you ever been lonely? Describe that experience.

Day 4. Sin Enters God's Perfect World. Genesis 3.

1. Why were Adam and Eve afraid to face God?

2. Have you ever lied or done something you were ashamed of and afraid to share? Try to tell about this experience.

Day 5. Story of Cain and Abel. Genesis 4:1-15.
1. Why was Cain's offering unacceptable to God?
2. Define jealousy.

This is not a pleasant feeling, but it is one we have all experienced. Describe a time when you felt jealous.

Day 6. Cain Is Sent Away. Genesis 4:16-26.
1. What happened to Cain?
2. Has there ever been a time in your life when you felt separated from God? Share this experience.

Special Activity: Creation
Using a large sheet of paper, have different family members draw pictures that each retell one day of the creation story.

Week 2

Key Memory Verse: "I am God Almighty; walk before me and be blameless"
(Genesis 17:1).

Day 1. Story of Noah. Genesis 7:1-10.

Noah is a descendant of Cain, living in a time when the world had turned its back on God. Noah is a righteous man before God and blameless among the people of his time.

1. Why did God choose Noah?

2. Look up the word *righteous* in the glossary. Is there someone in your life who might be described this way?

Day 2. The Flood. Genesis 7:11-24.

1. What was left on the earth after the flood?

2. God still had hope for creation. When have you wanted to wash away something that made you sad and start over again?

Day 3. The Rain Stops. Genesis 8:1-17.

1. How did Noah test the land to see if it was okay to leave the ark?

Who gave the final word for Noah to leave?

2. Noah trusted God. What are some different ways you must trust God with things unknown?

Day 4. The Promise. Genesis 8:18-22.

1. What was the first thing Noah did when he left the ark?

What promise did God make?

2. What security and comfort do you find from God's promise in verse 22?

God sealed his promise to never destroy the earth by flood again with the sign of the rainbow.

Day 5. God's Covenant with Abraham. Genesis 15.

1. What was God's covenant with Abraham?

Why do you think that God made it with him?

2. God *never* breaks a promise. Can you think of a promise that you have made and never broken? What was it?

Day 6. Isaac Is Born. Genesis 21:1-21; 22:17-18.

1. How was the promise of God fulfilled to both Abraham and Sarah in a single act?

2. God cares for all our needs. Describe a time when you have felt sad and alone and God has comforted you.

Many times God uses other people to help us. Sometimes he uses us to help others. Describe a time when you have comforted another person.

Week 3

Key Memory Verse: "I am with you and will watch over you wherever you go" (Genesis 28:15).

Day 1. Abraham Tested. Genesis 22:1-14.

1. Why did God test Abraham?

2. What helps you to trust someone?

Day 2. Abraham Blessed. Genesis 22:15-24.

1. Why did God bless Abraham?

2. What effect does God's promise to Abraham have on the world today?

Day 3. Isaac's Blessing. Genesis 27:1-29.

Abraham finds a wife, Rebekah, for his son Isaac. They have twin sons, Esau and Jacob. Esau is older.

1. In your own words tell the story of how Jacob tricked his father.

2. Why do you think God chooses imperfect people like Jacob to carry on his work?

Day 4. Esau Upset. Genesis 27:30-46.

1. Why was Esau upset?

2. Has there ever been a time in your family when you felt you weren't treated fairly? Share this experience.

Day 5. Jacob Flees. Genesis 28:1-9.

1. What was Isaac's command?
   Did Jacob follow it?

2. Esau was angry with his father and looked for ways to shock and anger him. Have you ever felt angry with someone and wanted to hurt him or her in return?

Day 6. Jacob's Dream. Genesis 28:10-22.

1. Tell about Jacob's dream.

2. How does God's promise to Jacob in verse 15 make you feel?

Week 4

Key Memory Verse: "God will surely come to your aid" (Genesis 50:25).

Day 1. Jacob Meets Esau. Genesis 33.

Once more Jacob struggles for a blessing, this time with God. As a result of his persistence, he gains the blessing and also a new name—Israel.

Jacob was married to Leah and Rachel. Their twelve male children become the foundation of the tribes of Israel. Their children are Reuben, Simon, Levi, Judah, Dan, Naphtali, Gad, Asher, Issachar, Zebulun, Dinah, Joseph and Benjamin.

1. What did Esau do to Jacob when they met?

2. Think of someone you have felt angry with and are holding a grudge against. How do you feel about that relationship?

Pray that God will heal this relationship and help you to become friends again with that person.

The children of Esau are known as Edomites.

Day 2. Joseph's Dreams. Genesis 37:1-11.

1. How did Joseph's dreams make his brothers feel? Why?

2. Tell about your most recent dream.

Day 3. Joseph Sold into Slavery. Genesis 37:12-36.

1. Tell the story of Joseph in your own words.

2. Describe a time when you have felt betrayed or let down by someone.

Day 4. Pharaoh's Dream. Genesis 41:1-36.

Joseph becomes well respected in Egypt until Potiphar's wife falsely accuses him of wrongdoing, and he is thrown into prison.

1. What was the meaning of Pharaoh's dream, according to Joseph?

2. Joseph had a special gift as the interpreter of dreams. Describe a special gift you might have.

Day 5. Joseph in Charge of Egypt. Genesis 41:37-57.

1. Why was Joseph put in charge of Egypt?

2. What is someone who is wise like?

Tell about a person you know who could be described this way.

Day 6. Joseph Makes Himself Known. Genesis 45.

Joseph's brothers come to Egypt seeking help because of the famine. They don't recognize Joseph, but they ask him for food, and he gives it to them.

1. Why did Joseph tell his brothers not to feel badly about having sold him into slavery?

2. God can bring good even when things appear very bad. Tell about an experience you've had in which God has taken a bad situation and made it good.

Joseph dies leaving the promise of God to the sons of Israel that they would be returned to the land that he promised to Abraham, Isaac and Jacob.

Week 5

Key Memory Verse: "I will take you as my own people, and I will be your God" (Exodus 6:7).

Day 1. Birth of Moses. Exodus 1:22—2:10.

The Israelite population grows so large in Egypt that the Pharaoh, fearful that they would take over, enslaves them. Exodus tells about God's delivery of the Hebrew people from slavery in Egypt, and their journey into the Sinai wilderness. Moses becomes a messenger from God when God gives them his laws for proper living and for worship.

1. How did Moses' mother save him after the Pharaoh had ordered all Hebrew male babies to be killed?

2. Can you think of a time when you have felt afraid and someone you love helped you to feel safe and warm? Share this experience.

Day 2. Moses Runs Away. Exodus 2:11-23.

1. Why did Moses run from the Pharaoh?

2. Even though this situation seems bad, God will work many wonders through Moses. Describe a situation in your life today that seems bad.

Pray that God can use this for good.

Day 3. The Burning Bush. Exodus 3:1-10.

1. Who appeared to Moses?

What was God concerned about?

2. Name a place where you felt the presence of God. Describe how it felt to you.

Day 4. Moses' Job. Exodus 3:11-22.

1. What did God want Moses to do?

How did he feel about it?

2. God is always faithful to us. When we doubt ourselves, we need never doubt God. Can you think of a job or responsibility you faced that just seemed too big to handle? Tell about what happened.

Day 5. God Promises Help. Exodus 6:1-13, 26-30.

1. What was God's promise?

2. God loves people so much that he has continued to express his love to us all through history. How does God make his love known to you?

Day 6. The Ten Plagues. Exodus 10:1-20.

To let Pharaoh know that he wants his people to be freed, God sends ten plagues to Egypt. These are:

1. *The plague of blood*
2. *The plague of frogs*
3. *The plague of gnats*
4. *The plague of flies*
5. *The plague on Egyptian livestock*
6. *The plague of boils*
7. *The plague of hail*
8. *The plague of locusts*
9. *The plague of darkness*
10. *The plague on the firstborn*

1. Why did God have Moses send the ten plagues over Egypt?

2. God never breaks a promise. What promise has God made to you?

Week 6

*Key Memory Verse: "The Lord will fight for you; you need only to be still"
(Exodus 14:14).*

Day 1. The Plague of Darkness. Exodus 10:21-29.
1. In your own words, describe the plague of darkness.
2. Look at verse 21. How can darkness be felt?

Have you ever experienced fear in the dark? Tell what it was
like.

Remember, God is always with you.

Day 2. The Passover. Exodus 12:1-20, 28-32.
1. What instructions did God give the Hebrew people to follow
that would insure their safety from the tenth plague?
2. Even today there are certain instructions for physical safety
that we must follow. List several of these you use daily as you
travel to work, school or play.

Day 3. Crossing the Red Sea. Exodus 14:13-31.
1. How did the Israelites cross the Red Sea?

Find a map (in your Bible or encyclopedia) that will show you
the path Moses took when he led the Hebrews out of Egypt.
2. Tell about a time when you were traveling someplace and
you thought it would take forever to get there because of the
obstacles you faced.

Day 4. Mount Sinai. Exodus 19.
God continues to provide for the Israelites with food in the form of manna, quail and water. Moses sets up a court system to take care of the disagreements that the people had with each other.
1. What did God tell Moses that he would do for the Israelites if they obeyed him?
2. What does God promise us in return for our trust and obedience?

Day 5. The Ten Commandments. Exodus 20.
1. Name from memory as many of the commandments as you can.
2. If you made a covenant (agreement, contract) between God and yourself, what would it say?

Day 6. Israelites Rebel. Exodus 32:1-26.
God gives the Israelites other laws and instructions about how to worship him.
1. How did the people sin against God?
2. Modern-day idols are things that consume our thoughts, our time, and our emotions. What things or interests in your life might be considered idols?
   To whom or what are you devoting your life?
   The people of Israel turned once more from sin to God and carried out his instructions.

Special Activity: Prayer Journal
Begin a family prayer journal. Decorate a notebook together. Record on a regular basis praises and prayer requests from all family members.

Week 7

Key Memory Verse: "The Lord bless you and keep you; the Lord make his face shine upon you and be gracious to you; the Lord turn his face toward you and give you peace" (Numbers 6:24-26).

Day 1. Keeping God's Law. Leviticus 18:1-5.

Leviticus shows us what kind of people God wanted the Israelites to be. The instructions given in Exodus continue as the laws dealing with Israel's life as a holy people are more defined.

1. What warning does God give to the Israelites?

2. Describe a situation when you felt pressured to compromise your Christian beliefs.

Day 2. Reward for Obedience. Leviticus 26:1-13.

1. What are some of the rewards that God promised the Israelites if they obeyed him?

2. Look at verse 12. What are some ways you can show that you belong to God?

Day 3. Punishment for Disobedience. Leviticus 26:14-26.

1. What are some of the things that God told the Israelites he would do to them if they disobeyed?

2. Would you be more careful not to sin if sin caused you to break out in a rash of purple spots? Why?

Following their release from captivity in Egypt, the Israelites wandered in the wilderness of Sinai for forty years. The book of Numbers records many instances of rebellion by the people against God during that time. As the people continue to wander in the wilderness, the Lord commands Moses to take a count of the whole Israelite community. The total number of all the men twenty years and up was 603,550.

Day 4. Following a Cloud. Numbers 9:15-23.
1. The tabernacle was the tent where God met his people. What did the position of the cloud tell the people?
2. In what ways does God speak to you?

Day 5. Complaining to God. Numbers 11.
1. What did the people complain about?
   What did God do?
2. It is easy to forget the wonderful things God does constantly. What prayer has God answered for you recently?

Day 6. Exploring Canaan. Numbers 13:26-33.
1. What were the people afraid of?
2. Tell about a time that you were afraid and God comforted you.

Week 8

Key Memory Verse: "Love the LORD your God with all your heart and with all your soul and with all your strength" (Deuteronomy 6:5).

Day 1. Israelites Rebel. Numbers 14:1-30.

1. How did God react to the Israelites' complaints?

2. Have you ever had to speak on someone else's behalf? Tell about it.

If you know of someone who is in need of help, pray that God will help that person.

Following their release from captivity in Egypt, the Israelites wandered in the wilderness of Sinai for forty years. During that time, there were many instances of rebellion by the people.

Day 2. God Is Near. Deuteronomy 4:1-14.

Deuteronomy tells about Moses' last efforts to help his beloved people follow God.

1. Why were the Jewish people so special?

2. What has God done to show you how special you are?

Day 3. No Other God. Deuteronomy 4:15-19, 25-40.

1. What is an idol?

2. What modern-day idols do you have?

Day 4. Don't Forget the Lord. Deuteronomy 8.

1. List at least two things Moses reminds the people that the

Lord did for them.

2. What things do you do to remind yourself of God's gracious nature and his kingship?

Day 5. Blessings for Obedience. Deuteronomy 28:1-14.

In what has the feel of a farewell address, Moses continues to recount the mighty acts of God, warn about temptations, and make an earnest appeal for loyalty to and love of God as a condition of life in the promised land.

1. What are some of the blessings that Moses told the Israelites they would have if they obeyed the Lord?

2. What are some blessings you receive when you obey and follow God?

Day 6. Curses for Israel's Disobedience. Deuteronomy 28:15-35.

1. What are some of the bad things that would happen if the Israelites disobeyed?

2. Are there any consequences for you if you are disobedient to God?

What are they?

Moses was prohibited from entering the promised land due to lack of faith (Numbers 20). Before Moses' death, the Lord commissioned Joshua to lead the Israelites into the promised land. Of the original males of military age who left Egypt, only Joshua and Caleb survived to enter the promised land.

Part 2
History Books

Joshua
Judges
Ruth
1 Samuel
2 Samuel
1 Kings
2 Kings
1 Chronicles
2 Chronicles
Ezra
Nehemiah
Esther

Week 9

*Key Memory Verse: "Now fear the Lord and serve him with all faithfulness"
(Joshua 24:14).*

Day 1. Be Strong and Courageous. Joshua 1:1-11.
*The book of Joshua describes Moses' death and God's selection of
Joshua as a leader of his people. The land that God promised the
Israelites is occupied by the Canaanite people. Using God's direction,
Joshua prepares the wandering tribes of Israel to conquer Palestine and
claim it as the promised land.*
1. How does Joshua respond to what God commands him to
do?
2. How does knowing God is with you help you to be strong
in hard times?

Day 2. Rahab and the Spies. Joshua 2.
1. What was so special about Rahab?
2. Rahab took a chance. Have you ever taken a chance for
God? Describe your experience.

Day 3. Jericho. Joshua 5:13—6:27.
1. Tell about the fall of Jericho.
2. This was a lesson in trust and obedience. What is trust?

  Is there a person in your life you trust more than others?
Describe that person.

Day 4. Achan's Sin. Joshua 7.
1. How did Achan sin?
2. Do we have to be killed for our sin?
   How does God deal with our sin?

Day 5. The Israelites Are Tricked. Joshua 9.
1. How did the Gibeonites trick the Israelites?
2. Think of a time when you were tricked or lied to. Why might a person lie?

Day 6. The Covenant Renewed. Joshua 24:14-33.
The Israelites continue their military campaign against the Canaanites. Many fierce battles are waged and won with God leading his people to a final victory. The land is divided among the twelve tribes.
1. What did Joshua remind the Israelite people to do?
2. What can we do to keep our hearts faithful to God?

Week 10

Key Memory Verse: "Where you go I will go, and where you stay I will stay. Your people will be my people and your God my God" (Ruth 1:16).

Day 1. God Calls Gideon. Judges 6:1-13.

Judges covers two hundred years following Israel's entry into Canaan. This book vividly portrays warfare at its lowest. The writer shows that loyalty to God is necessary for national success and disloyalty guarantees disaster.

The Israelites continue to fight to maintain their presence in Palestine and conquer surrounding territories. The "judges" are leaders from the twelve tribes who exercise authority under God in both military and civil matters.

1. Why were the Israelites calling out to God for help?

2. Has there ever been a time in your life when you doubted God's love for you? Explain.

Day 2. Gideon's Sign. Judges 6:14-40.

1. Why did Gideon ask God to give him different signs as proof that he was supposed to save Israel?

2. What proof does God give you that he loves you?

What proof do you give your family that you love them?

Day 3. Gideon's Victory. Judges 7.

1. Why did God want Gideon to have a smaller army?

2. It is easy for people to claim credit for something God has accomplished. Some even call it "chance" or "coincidence." Tell about something that happened in your life that was so extraordinary that only God could have done it.

Day 4. Samson and Delilah. Judges 16:1-22.

Once again the Israelites rebel against God and are conquered by their enemy, the Philistines. For forty years they lived under their rule. Then a hero to the people named Samson is born.

1. What was the secret of Samson's strength?

2. Name two special strengths you have. Name two weaknesses you see in yourself. Write these four things on a piece of paper. After exchanging papers, praise God for the strengths of one another, listing them individually. Now pray that God can help each of you to grow beyond your weaknesses.

Day 5. Samson's Death. Judges 16:23-31.

1. How did Samson get his strength back?

2. God continues to love us even when we fail him. Write a short prayer praising God for his constant love.

Day 6. Naomi and Ruth. Ruth 1.

The book of Ruth tells a story of love and courage.

1. How did Ruth show her love and loyalty to her mother-in-law?

2. In what ways do your family members show love and loyalty to each other?

Ruth eventually married Boaz, who is her nearest relative. Much of our insight into the customs of ancient Israel comes from this four-chapter book. Ruth's great-grandson, David, later became one of Israel's greatest kings.

Old Testament Rulers and Prophets

The kingdoms of Israel and Judah were united for 120 years and divided for over 200 years. Then Jerusalem was destroyed and Israel was held in captivity again. Judah lasted alone for another 125 years.

The following chart shows the number of years each of the kings of Israel and Judah reigned, as well as the time period that each prophet served in.

United Kingdom

Saul	40 years
David	40 years
Solomon	40 years

Divided Kingdom

Kings of Israel Northern Kingdom		Prophets	Kings of Judah Southern Kingdom	
Jeroboam	22 years		Rehoboam	17 years
			Abijah	3 years
			Asa	41 years
Nadab	2 years			
Baasha	24 years			
Elah	2 years			
Zimri	7 days			
Omri	12 years			
Ahab	22 years	Elijah	Jehoshaphat	25 years
Ahaziah	2 years			
Joram	12 years			
		Elisha	Jehoram	8 years
			Ahaziah	1 year
			Athaliah	7 years
Jehu	28 years			
			Joash	40 years
Jehoahaz	17 years			
Jehoash	16 years			
			Amaziah	29 years
Jeroboam II	41 years	Jonah	Azariah	52 years
		Amos		

Kings of Israel Northern Kingdom		Prophets	Kings of Judah Southern Kingdom	
Zechariah	6 months			
Shallum	1 month			
Menahem	10 years			
Pekahiah	2 years			
Pekah	20 years			
		Hosea Isaiah Micah	Jotham	16 years
			Ahaz	16 years
Hoshea	9 years			
			Hezekiah	29 years
The fall of Samaria/ Assyrian captivity in 722 B.C.			Manasseh	55 years
		Zephaniah	Amon	2 years
			Josiah	31 years
		Jeremiah	Jehoahaz	3 months
			Jehoiakim	11 years
			Jehoiachin	3 months
		Ezekiel Daniel	Zedekiah	11 years

Destruction of Jerusalem/
second Babylonian
captivity in 586 B.C.

Week 11

Key Memory Verse: "For the sake of his great name the LORD will not reject his people, because the LORD was pleased to make you his own" (1 Samuel 12:22).

Day 1. God Calls Samuel. 1 Samuel 3.

First Samuel creates a bridge between the period of the judges and Israel's first king. Samuel, who would become the last "judge" of Israel, is born to Hannah.

1. What did Eli tell Samuel to do when the Lord called his name again?

2. In order to answer God's call we must first be silent. Then we must listen for and recognize God's voice. What do you hear God calling you to?

If you feel you have no call as yet, what do you think the silence means?

Day 2. Samuel Anoints David. 1 Samuel 16:1-13.

God calls Samuel as a prophet and later becomes the last "judge" of Israel. As he advances in years, the tribes of Israel are being pressed by their enemy, the Philistines. The tribes need strong leadership, but Samuel is growing old so they demand a king. God then appoints Saul, a brave warrior and a man of wealth, as the first king of Israel.

1. What did the Lord tell Samuel that he looks at in a person?

2. How do you judge people?

What three words can you use to describe what is "in your heart"?

Day 3. David Serves Saul. 1 Samuel 16:14-23.
1. Why was Saul pleased with David?

2. What things help to make you feel relaxed and peaceful?

Day 4. David and Goliath. 1 Samuel 17:1-37.
1. What did Goliath shout daily to the Israelites?

2. Sometimes our problems seem as big as giants. What lesson does David teach us about handling these problems?

Day 5. The Battle. 1 Samuel 17:38-58.
1. How was David able to win?

2. David knew he wasn't alone as he faced Goliath. Who faces life with you?

Day 6. David and Jonathan. 1 Samuel 20.
Saul becomes increasingly jealous of David and plans to kill him.

1. How did Jonathan show his great friendship toward David?

2. Have you ever had to choose between family and friends, or between two friends? Explain.

The rest of the book shows David establishing himself as a military leader. Saul and his sons are killed in battle.

Week 12

Key Memory Verse: "It is God who arms me with strength and makes my way perfect. He makes my feet like the feet of a deer; he enables me to stand on the heights" (2 Samuel 22:33-34).

Day 1. Israel's New King. 2 Samuel 5:1-10.

Second Samuel gives the account of the reign of David as he seeks to unify the nation of Israel.

1. How did David become powerful?

2. The word *covenant* means agreement or contract. Discuss an agreement you have in your home. (Who are the parties? What are the conditions? What are the promises?)

Day 2. David Defeats the Philistines. 2 Samuel 5:17-25.

1. Who helped David win?

   How did he help?

2. Think of a time you were in a fight. How did you feel? (Were you angry, scared or upset?)

Day 3. The Ark of God. 2 Samuel 6:1-5.

You might want to read Exodus 25:10-22 to learn about the ark of the covenant. Remember, the ark is very holy and contains the commandments.

1. What did David do while returning the ark to his people?

   Why did he act this way?

2. How do you act when you feel very happy and want to celebrate?

Day 4. Nathan Confronts David. 2 Samuel 12:1-10.

God makes a covenant with David that insures lasting leadership for Israel. But then David sees a beautiful woman (Bathsheba) who is married to one of his soldiers. Even though he knows it is wrong, he has sex with her. Then he sends her husband to the front of the battle lines where he is killed.

1. What did David do that was wrong?

2. Have you ever taken something that does not belong to you? Talk about what that was like.

Bathsheba and David got married and had a son—Solomon. At the end of the book, David ran for his life from the armies of his son Absalom, who took over as king of Jerusalem. Absalom was later killed in battle, and David was restored as king.

Day 5. Solomon Is King. 1 Kings 1:28-40.

First Kings begins with the account of the reign of Solomon and, following his death, the division of the united kingdom into north and south kingdoms.

1. What was Solomon made ruler over?

2. Being king means taking a lot of responsibility. What do you think it would be like to be king?

Day 6. Solomon Asks for Wisdom. 1 Kings 3:1-15.

1. What were some of the gifts God gave to Solomon?

   Why did God give Solomon all these gifts?

2. Name five things you consider good and five things you consider evil. Discuss these things.

Week 13

Key Memory Verse: "But your hearts must be fully committed to the LORD our God, to live by his decrees and obey his commands, as at this time" (1 Kings 8:61).

Day 1. Solomon's Wisdom. 1 Kings 4:29-34.

1. Describe different ways in which Solomon was wise.

2. When has someone asked you for advice?

Giving advice carries with it serious responsibility. If a person you have advised ends up in trouble or is hurt as a result of your advice, is it his or her responsibility or yours? Explain your answer.

Day 2. Building the Temple. 1 Kings 6. (Preschool: 1 Kings 6:1-6, 37-38)

To help picture the size of the temple, remember that a cubit is about 18-22 inches.

1. What struck you as the most interesting fact about the temple?

2. Think about your own house. What room do you like the most? Why?

Day 3. Bringing in the Ark. 1 Kings 8:1-21.

1. When the priests placed the ark in the temple, what very special event took place?

2. At a wedding the beautiful dress, the flowers, the ring and the vows are all things included in the ceremony to symbolize the couple's love and loyalty to one another. In the same way in this passage the setting, the sacrifices and everything else was in perfect order according to God's instruction. What do you think the people were trying to communicate to God?

Day 4. Prayer of Dedication. 1 Kings 8:22-24, 54-61.
1. Name three characteristics of God found in verse 22.
2. List three things about yourself you are most proud of.

Day 5. The Lord Appears to Solomon. 1 Kings 9:1-9.
1. What did God tell Solomon he needed to do?
2. What happens when children don't obey their parents' rules, or adults don't obey society's rules?
Describe two rules you feel are important.

Day 6. Israel Rebels. 1 Kings 12:1-17.
Against the instructions of God, Solomon marries women of foreign religions. This includes seven hundred wives of royal birth and three hundred concubines. These women introduce Solomon to the worship of gods and idols to Solomon. As Solomon grows old, he turns his heart to these gods and sins against the Lord. Solomon's lack of faithfulness results in God's judgment as the nation splits apart.

The two tribes in the south remain loyal to Solomon's son Rehoboam and are called Judah. Ten tribes follow Solomon's servant's son, Jeroboam, to form a nation in the north called Israel.

1. Who did King Rehoboam go to for advice?
2. Listening to the advice of others can be a good thing, but listening to the wrong person can get us into trouble. Name two people whom you would trust for advice. Discuss why.

Week 14

Key Memory Verse: "Do not forget the covenant I have made with you, and do not worship other gods. Rather, worship the LORD your God" (2 Kings 17:38-39).

Day 1. Elijah, Prophet of Israel. 1 Kings 17.

1. Do you think the widow had a strong faith in God? Why?

2. Many situations appear hopeless to us, but we know that God is faithful even in those times. Discuss a seemingly hopeless situation in your family and pray for one another now.

Day 2. Elijah and Obadiah. 1 Kings 18:1-16.

The prophets, Elijah and Elisha, appear at a critical crossroad in the history of Israel—just as King Ahab is changing the official religion from worship of God to worship of Baal, a false god.

1. What great thing had Obadiah done?

2. It is sometimes hard not to do things that everyone else is doing. We are afraid we won't fit in. Discuss one thing you feel pressured to do but feel uncomfortable about doing.

Day 3. Elijah on Mount Carmel. 1 Kings 18:17-46.

1. How did Elijah expose Baal, the alleged god of weather?

2. Advertisements tell us that wearing the right clothes or using the right deodorant will make us happy and successful. These are false claims. Discuss other things or products that make false claims.

What makes you feel successful and happy?

Day 4. Elijah Taken Up to Heaven. 2 Kings 2:1-15.
Second Kings continues the record of the newly divided nation of Israel through the exile of the Israelites to Babylon.
1. What was Elisha's request of Elijah before he left?
2. Think of one person whom you really admire. What are three qualities about this person you would most like to have?

Day 5. Elisha's Miracle. 2 Kings 5:1-14.
1. Tell how Naaman was healed of leprosy.
2. Naaman wanted God to be conjured up and his healing to appear more dramatic. Naaman found healing not through "magic" but through obedience. God is always present, not just when we "call" on him. Talk about how God is present in your world.

Day 6. The Last King of Israel. 2 Kings 17:1-23.
The majority of the rulers continued to be evil and lead the two kingdoms away from God.
1. Why did Israel lose the battle against Assyria?
2. The Israelites broke their covenant with God. God still loved them but God never breaks a covenant, so they had to suffer the consequences. Discuss the spoken and unspoken agreements in your family.

Do the consequences of breaking the rules seem fair?

Week 15

Key Memory Verse: "Give thanks to the LORD, for he is good; his love endures forever" (1 Chronicles 16:34).

Day 1. The Book of the Law Found. 2 Kings 22:1-13.

1. Why was Judah's king, Josiah, upset when he heard what was written in the Book of the Law?

2. Share an experience when you were in trouble because you did not know the rules.

How could things have been different?

Day 2. Josiah Renews the Covenant. 2 Kings 22:14—23:3.

1. Why did God protect the people of Judah?

2. Look up the word *mercy* in the glossary. Describe a time when you showed mercy to another person.

How does God show us mercy?

Nebuchadnezzar, king of Babylon, marched against Jerusalem with his whole army. Jerusalem eventually fell and the people of the Southern Kingdom, Judah, were sent into Babylon as captives.

Day 3. God's Promise to David. 1 Chronicles 17:1-15.

First Chronicles records Israel's genealogical history, with special attention given to the life of David. Similar information on the history of Israel is presented in Samuel, Kings and Chronicles. A basic difference being that Samuel and Kings are addressing the people in captivity in Babylon, and Chronicles later addresses those people who are returning to the promised land.

1. What was God's promise to David?

2. God has made many promises to us. Discuss a promise that you would like to make to God.

Day 4. David's Prayer. 1 Chronicles 17:16-27.

1. What did David want other men to say about God?

2. What three words would you like people to use when describing you?

Day 5. King Jehoshaphat's Prayer. 2 Chronicles 20:1-12.

Second Chronicles records the history of the rulers of Judah and focuses on God's special relationship with the Israelites.

1. What did King Jehoshaphat and his people do when they heard that a large army was coming to fight them?

2. Share something you fear in your life right now. Take a few moments to pray for one another.

Day 6. Jehoshaphat Defeats Moab and Ammon. 2 Chronicles 20:13-30.

(Preschool: 2 Chronicles 20:13-17, 26-30)

1. Tell how the Israelites defeated the Moabites and Ammonites.

2. Think of an object or a situation that makes you feel threatened (afraid and unsafe). Discuss ways that God helps you overcome your fear.

Week 16

Key Memory Verse: "With praise and thanksgiving they sang to the LORD: 'He is good; his love to Israel endures forever' " (Ezra 3:11).

Day 1. Invitation to the Passover. 2 Chronicles 30:1-9.

1. How did the king try to encourage people to come celebrate the Passover?

2. What special days do you celebrate in your church?

Describe some traditions that make those days more meaningful.

Day 2. The Passover Celebration. 2 Chronicles 30:10-27.

1. Why was there great joy in Jerusalem?

2. When you go away on vacation, what do you miss most about being away from home?

What are some of the first things you do when you return home?

Day 3. Sennacherib Threatens Jerusalem. 2 Chronicles 32:1-23.

(Preschool: 2 Chronicles 32:1-8, 22-23)

1. Who did Sennacherib and his officers speak out against?

What happened to Sennacherib and his men?

2. At times our problems seem too big for us to handle. Share a present or past problem when you felt God's presence enabled you to solve or resolve the situation.

Day 4. Hezekiah's Life. 2 Chronicles 32:24-33.

1. Name one thing about King Hezekiah that stands out to you.

2. Read verse 25 again. What is wrong with false pride?

Day 5. The Fall of Jerusalem. 2 Chronicles 36:15-23.

1. How long did the Jewish people remain captives in Babylon?

2. Share an experience in your life when you were warned that something would hurt you, but you ignored the warning and did it anyway.

What were some of the consequences?

Day 6. The Exiles Return. Ezra 1.

Ezra gives an account of a new beginning for God's people as they return to Jerusalem from exile in Babylon. As a priest and teacher of the Law, Ezra sees that the temple is rebuilt and the worship practices of the Jewish people are purified.

1. Who helped the Jewish people return to their homeland?

2. If your house were to somehow be destroyed, which room would you want to rebuild first? Why?

Week 17

Key Memory Verse: "Blessed be your glorious name, and may it be exalted above all blessing and praise. You alone are the LORD. You made the heavens, even the highest heavens, and all their starry host, the earth and all that is on it, the seas and all that is in them. You give life to everything, and the multitudes of heaven worship you" (Nehemiah 9:5-6).

Day 1. Rebuilding the Temple. Ezra 3.

(Preschool: Ezra 3:1-3, 6-7, 10-13)

1. How did the people contribute to the building of the temple?

How did the people show their feelings about the rebuilt temple?

2. Reflect on a project that your entire family worked on together. What positive things resulted from your efforts?

Day 2. Nehemiah's Request. Nehemiah 2:1-10.

Nehemiah tells of the efforts to rebuild the walls of Jerusalem and to restore the religious institutions and practices of the Hebrew people. As cupbearer to King Artaxerxes, Nehemiah is able to use his influence to persuade the king to give his blessing in this endeavor.

1. What does Nehemiah ask the king for?

2. In verse 5 Nehemiah shot an "arrow prayer" to God asking him for help while in the middle of a conversation with the king. Tell about a time that you shot a quick "arrow prayer" to God asking for help.

When can you use "arrow prayers"?

Day 3. Inspecting Jerusalem's Walls. Nehemiah 2:11-20.

1. Why did Nehemiah want to rebuild the wall?

2. Have you ever done something that was not the popular thing to do, but you felt you had to? Describe your experience.

Day 4. Ezra Reads the Law. Nehemiah 8.

(Preschool: Nehemiah 8:1-6, 8-11)

1. What were the people doing while the Law was being read to them?

What did Nehemiah tell them to do?

2. Verse 10 says, "for the joy of the LORD is your strength." What does that mean to you?

Day 5. The King's Edict. Esther 3:13—4:8.

Esther is a lovely young Jewish woman who was reared by her cousin Mordecai. At the command of the king, she and many other maidens are taken to the king's palace and placed in his harem.

1. Why was Mordecai so upset?

2. How do you express your feelings when you are very upset?

Day 6. Esther's Plan. Esther 4:9-17.

1. How did Esther intend to risk her life?

2. Have you ever had to stand up on someone else's behalf? Describe this experience.

Later in the book we see Esther and Mordecai foil the plot to destroy the Jews. As a result, they are highly regarded by both the king and the Jewish people.

Part 3
Books of Poetry

Job
Psalms
Proverbs
Ecclesiastes
Song of Songs

Week 18

Key Memory Verse: "He performs wonders that cannot be fathomed, miracles that cannot be counted" (Job 5:9).

Day 1. An Upright Man. Job 1:1-12.

Job is the story of a righteous man whose faith sustains him through overwhelming adversity. The story aims at probing the depths of faith in spite of suffering.

1. What kind of a person was Job?

What did Satan tell God that Job would do if bad things happened to him?

2. Share a situation when you feel you were having "bad things" happen to you.

Describe your reactions to these "bad things."

Day 2. Job's First Test. Job 1:13-22.

1. What bad things happened to Job?

2. What is the most unfair thing that ever happened to you?

How did it affect your thoughts about God?

Day 3. Job's Second Test. Job 2:1-10.

1. How did Job respond to God after all his tests?

2. How do you respond to God when life seems difficult?

Day 4. Job's Poem of Wisdom. Job 28:20-28.

1. How does Job define wisdom and understanding?

2. Tell about a decision that you made which reflects the kind of understanding Job was talking about.

Day 5. The Lord Answers Job. Job 38.
(Preschool: Job 38:1-7, 34-41)
1. Who was asking all of the questions?
   What were they about?
2. If you were in Job's place, what kind of answers would you have wanted from God?

Day 6. Job Responds. Job 42.
(Preschool: Job 42:1-7, 10, 15-17)
1. How did God bless Job even more than he had in the beginning?
2. Each experience in life, good or bad, leaves us with more than what we had in the beginning. Think of something in your life now that appears to be bad. Can you think of at least two good things that may come out of this?

Week 19

Key Memory Verse: "The LORD gives strength to his people; the LORD blesses his people with peace" (Psalm 29:11).

Day 1. David's Discouragement. Psalm 13.

Psalms is a book of prayer, song and poetry expressing a full range of human emotions. Through their prayers, the authors show us how to relate to God.

1. Why does David say he will sing to the Lord?

2. Describe a time you felt God had forgotten you.

Day 2. Perfect Harmony. Psalm 19.

1. Read verse 14 again. What does it mean to you?

2. State an attribute or quality of God, such as "God is good." The person next to you will repeat what you said and add a new quality, for instance "God is good and wonderful." Continue around the group.

Day 2. The Shepherd Song. Psalm 23.

1. How is the Lord like a shepherd to us?

2. Close your eyes for a moment and think of the most beautiful place you can imagine. Describe this place aloud.

Special Activity: Psalm 23

Memorize a verse a day from Psalm 23.

Day 3. Confidence in Trouble. Psalm 27.

(Preschool: Psalm 27:1-2, 11-14)

1. Why is David so confident in this psalm?
2. What kind of trouble are you facing in your life today?
   Pray for confidence and courage.

Day 4. The Great Confession. Psalm 51.

1. Who did David sin against?
2. Look up the word *sin* in the glossary and discuss it.
   Tell about a time when you sinned against God.

Day 5. Worshiping God. Psalm 84.

1. Where would the psalmist rather be?
2. Tell how it feels to be with someone you love very much.

Day 6. God's Benefits. Psalm 103.

1. What are some of the things the writer says God does for us?
2. What can you add to this list?

Week 20

Key Memory Verse: "Trust in the LORD with all your heart and lean not on your own understanding" (Proverbs 3:5).

Day 1. Remembering God's Work. Psalm 106:1-23, 44-48.

1. In these verses the writer is remembering all the things that God did for the people. Which of these stories do you remember reading?

2. Tell about a time from your own history when God helped you do something difficult.

Day 2. God's Care. Psalm 139.

(Preschool: Psalm 139:1-18)

1. What are some of the things God knows about us?

2. To find out how well you know your family, guess these things about each other: favorite color, favorite dessert, favorite time of year, and favorite way to have fun.

Day 3. The Way of Wisdom. Proverbs 4.

(Preschool: Proverbs 4:1-9, 24-27)

Proverbs is a collection of writings that offers practical wisdom for everyday living.

1. What does the father want his son to do?

2. What is the best advice you have ever received?

Day 4. Warnings Against Doing Wrong. Proverbs 6:12-22.

1. Name seven things that God hates.

2. Share seven things that you think are wrong to do.

Day 5. Proverbs of Solomon. Proverbs 10.

(Preschool: Proverbs 10:1-19)

1. What does Solomon say about love?

2. If "love covers over all wrongs," is it okay to go ahead and offend people?

How does love change your actions toward others?

Day 6. Honest Speech. Proverbs 12:6, 14, 17-19, 22, 25.

1. What are the good things that words do?

What are the bad things?

2. If you could take back one thing you have said to someone, what would it be? Why?

Week 21

Key Memory Verse: "Everything God does will endure forever; nothing can be added to it and nothing taken from it" (Ecclesiastes 3:14).

Day 1. Rich and Poor. Proverbs 19:1-17.

1. How does God want us to treat people who have less than us?

2. Think of someone you know who seems less fortunate. How can you show God's love to that person?

Day 2. Noble Character. Proverbs 31:10-31.

1. Describe the woman these verses tell about.

2. This woman has many good qualities that both men and women want to have. How would you like to be more like her?

Day 3. A Time for Everything. Ecclesiastes 3:1-14.

Ecclesiastes describes the meaninglessness and despair of life without God.

1. What other categories can you add to verses 1-8?

2. What "time" is it in your life?

Day 4. Riches. Ecclesiastes 5:8-20.

1. Why does the author say, "Whoever loves money never has money enough" (v. 10)?

2. What does money mean to you?

Day 5. Fear God. Ecclesiastes 12:9-14.
1. What does the author say is his conclusion?

2. What are some things about God that you fear?

Day 6. A Gazelle and a Dove. Song of Songs 2.

Song of Songs expresses love and relationship in beautiful poetic form.

1. Name three different things the bride in this poem compares her love to.

2. Think about someone you love. What animal would you compare that person to? Why?

Part 4
Prophets

Isaiah

Jeremiah

Lamentations

Ezekiel

Daniel

Hosea

Joel

Amos

Obadiah

Jonah

Micah

Nahum

Habakkuk

Zephaniah

Haggai

Zechariah

Malachi

Week 22

Day 1. Rebellious Judah. Isaiah 1:10-20.

Isaiah, a prophet of God, analyzes the failures of the Israelite nation and offers hope for the future.

1. Why does God reject Judah's sacrifice?

2. In what ways do people practice religion without having a real relationship to God?

Day 2. Isaiah's Commission. Isaiah 6.

1. Tell how Isaiah was called by God to become a prophet.

2. How has God shown you that you are special and "set apart"?

What message do you feel God has for you to tell your friends and family?

Day 3. Fear God. Isaiah 8:11-22.

1. Who are the people turning to for advice?

2. Who do you go to when you need advice? Why?

Day 4. A Child Is Born. Isaiah 9:2-7.

In this passage the prophet Isaiah appears to be telling about the birth of Christ which will come.

1. According to these verses, what will the one who comes do?

2. In whom or what do you place your hope for the future? Why?

Day 5. Root of Jesse. Isaiah 11:1-9.

This appears to be another prophecy about Christ's coming.

1. Name six features of the Spirit of the Lord.

2. How do you see the Spirit of the Lord at work in your life?

Day 6. A Song of Praise. Isaiah 25.

Isaiah continues in his role as prophet and speaks God's judgment against the nations threatening the borders of Judah. Israel is also warned of the coming judgment of the Lord because of their sin and rebellion.

1. What is promised in verses 6-8?

2. If there is "no more sadness," what other things would be gone as well? (Would there be sickness? death?)

Week 23

Key Memory Verse: "Fear not, for I have redeemed you; I have summoned you by name; you are mine" (Isaiah 43:1).

Day 1. Look to God. Isaiah 31.

1. Why are the people of Israel told not to look to the Egyptians for help?

2. Who do you rely on for help?

Day 2. Comfort for God's People. Isaiah 40:1-14.

The tone of Isaiah changes as the author gives comfort and hope to the people. He looks forward to exiled Judah being restored to Palestine.

1. What stands forever? Explain.

2. What security does verse 8 give for us today?

Day 3. Comfort for God's People. Isaiah 40:15-31.

1. Tell two or more things that you learned about God from this.

2. Talk about a time when God has given you extra strength when you needed it.

Day 4. God's Ultimate Plan. Isaiah 52.

(Preschool: Isaiah 52:1-10)

1. Who is the servant in verses 13-15?

2. Think of some good news you received recently. How did you hear of it?

Day 5. The Suffering Servant. Isaiah 53.

(Preschool: Isaiah 53:1-6)

1. Find five or more words in this chapter that parallel the description of Jesus' suffering and glory.

2. Have you ever taken the blame for something someone else did? Why? Share this experience.

Day 6. Comfort from God. Isaiah 55.

(Preschool: Isaiah 55:1-3, 12-13)

1. Look closely at verses 10-11. What do you think God's purpose is? How will God accomplish his purpose?

2. Look up *purpose* in the glossary. Describe what you feel is your "purpose" on earth right now. How will you go about accomplishing this purpose?

Special Activity: Thank You, God

Write your own poem or prayer to God thanking him for who he is and for what he does for you.

Week 24

Key Memory Verse: "Before I formed you in the womb I knew you, before you were born I set you apart; I appointed you as a prophet to the nations" (Jeremiah 1:5).

Day 1. Israel Forsakes God. Jeremiah 2:1-19.

Jeremiah portrays the Israelite nation threatened, conquered and finally led into exile by the Babylonians.

1. How did the Israelites rebel against God?

2. To us it seems silly to worship a god made of wood, but we still worship false gods. What things in your life demand most, if not all, of your energy, money, time and loyalty?

Day 2. Idols. Jeremiah 2:20-37.

1. What did the Israelites say about the wooden idols?

2. Think of the last time you (adults and children) disobeyed your parents. What were the consequences? How did you feel?

Day 3. God's Promise of Restoration. Jeremiah 31:1-22.

Jeremiah focuses on rewards and punishment, faithfulness and disobedience. He criticizes Judah for worshiping foreign gods and calls the people to return to God. Their sin will be judged, but a new and more enduring relationship with God will follow.

1. What were some of the promises that God made to the Israelites before they were to be taken from their homeland?

2. When you punish someone, what spoken and unspoken promises can you offer?

How can you love someone and still punish him or her?

Day 4. A New Covenant. Jeremiah 31:23-40; 32:40.
1. What is the new covenant that God promises the Israelites?
2. Showing kindness is a good thing, whether you live in Los Angeles or in an African village. Why do you think this is so?

Day 5. Thrown into a Cistern. Jeremiah 38:1-13.
Jeremiah was falsely accused of deserting the Babylonians, so he was thrown into prison.
1. How was Jeremiah saved?
2. Think of a situation you were in when you felt afraid you were going to be hurt. How were you saved?

Day 6. Jeremiah Questioned. Jeremiah 38:14-28.
1. What was Jeremiah's message for King Zedekiah?
2. Sometimes it is best to surrender when the opposition is too great. Surrender does not always mean giving up or admitting defeat. Surrender sometimes simply means changing the game plan or strategy, but still moving ahead with what you believe. What are some alternatives to surrender?

Week 25

Key Memory Verse: "The LORD is good to those whose hope is in him, to the one who seeks him; it is good to wait quietly for the salvation of the LORD" (Lamentations 3:25-26).

Day 1. Bitter Grief and Quiet Hope. Lamentations 3:1-24.

(Preschool: Lamentations 3:1-6, 19-24)

Lamentations consists of five poems of sorrow. These poems express the sadness of the Jewish people at the fall of Jerusalem, the destruction of the temple, and the scattering of the people under the conquering Babylonians in 586 B.C.

1. Read aloud two sentences showing grief and two sentences showing hope.

2. Tell about a time when you felt very sad.

What or who comforts you when you are sad?

Day 2. Waiting Upon the Lord. Lamentations 3:25-66.

1. Who is the Lord good to? (Read the verse aloud.)

2. Waiting for something can be hard. What are some things you have to wait for everyday?

How do you wait for the Lord?

Day 3. Majestic Vision. Ezekiel 1.

(Preschool: Ezekiel 1:1-7, 26-28)

Ezekiel, a prophet to the exiles, assures his hearers of the abiding presence of God among them through a mixture of visions, messages, dramas and poems.

1. Name at least one thing that impressed you about the creatures and the glory of God.

2. Describe the most beautiful sight you have ever seen.

Day 4. Ezekiel's Call. Ezekiel 2.

1. What did God want Ezekiel to do?

2. Can you remember a time when you were asked to choose
between doing right or following the crowd? Share this.

Day 5. The Scroll. Ezekiel 3:1-15.

(Preschool: Ezekiel 3:1-7, 12-15)

1. What did God want Ezekiel to say to the Israelites?

2. Who are the people who speak for the Lord today?
   How do they speak for God?

Day 6. Warning to Israel. Ezekiel 3:16-27.

(Preschool: Ezekiel 3:16-17, 22-27)

1. Why did God make Ezekiel into a watchman for the Israelites?

2. Imagine there was a terrible storm that washed a bridge
away, and you were the first person to the bridge, and you saw
the danger. Should you stay and warn the other cars or let
everyone take their chances? Why?

   How does knowledge make us responsible?

Week 26

Key Memory Verse: "Praise be to the name of God for ever and ever; wisdom and power are his" (Daniel 2:20).

Day 1. Siege of Jerusalem. Ezekiel 4.

(Preschool: Ezekiel 4:1-8)

1. How many days did Ezekiel have to lie on his left side and on his right side?

What did each day represent?

2. Give examples of symbols we use every day. (For example, what do the numbers on the clock represent? Or the numbers on a calendar?)

Day 2. Valley of Dry Bones. Ezekiel 37:1-14.

1. Who did the dry bones represent?

2. God can do the impossible in our lives. Tell about a situation in your life that is uncertain or stressful.

Pray about this together.

Day 3. One Nation. Ezekiel 37:15-28.

1. What did God tell Ezekiel that he was going to do for the Israelites?

2. How can you be a peacemaker in your family?

Pray for our world leaders and their efforts toward peace.

Day 4. Daniel's Training. Daniel 1.

Daniel, through stories and visions, prophesies the future and recounts an exiled person's courage and loyalty to God.

King Nebuchadnezzar makes Daniel ruler over the entire province of Babylon and places him in charge of all its wise men.

1. What did Daniel ask permission to do regarding proper food?

How did the changed menu affect the four young men?

2. If you were asked to do something that you know is against God's will, how would you respond?

Day 5. Image of Gold. Daniel 3:1-7.

1. What did King Nebuchadnezzar command the people to do?

What was the punishment for disobeying Nebuchadnezzar?

2. What kind of punishment do you fear the most?

Have you ever experienced that punishment?

Day 6. Fiery Furnace. Daniel 3:8-30.

1. What happened to Shadrach, Meshach and Abednego? Why?

2. Verses 16-18 give us an example of unconditional loyalty and obedience. Look up "unconditional" in the glossary. What condition do you place on your loyalty and obedience to God? Why?

Week 27

Key Memory Verse: "The ways of the LORD are right; the righteous walk in them, but the rebellious stumble in them" (Hosea 14:9).

Day 1. The Writing on the Wall. Daniel 5:1-9.

1. Why was King Belshazzar so frightened?

2. Describe a time when you were very frightened.

Tell how you felt and in what ways your feelings were showing.

Day 2. Daniel's Interpretation. Daniel 5:10-31.

(Preschool: Daniel 5:10-17, 24-30)

1. What did Daniel say the writing on the wall meant?

2. In what ways have you been warned about the life you lead? Who warned you?

Day 3. The Decree. Daniel 6:1-9.

1. What was the only area of Daniel's life that King Darius' administrators could find fault with?

2. What is an area of your life that people might find fault with?

Day 4. In the Lion's Den. Daniel 6:10-28.

1. Why was Daniel saved from the lions?

2. Look at verse 24 again. Our actions usually affect many others around us, especially our families. Tell about a time when the actions of one member of your family affected the whole family.

Day 5. The Sins of Israel. Hosea 8.

Hosea depicts Israel's unfaithfulness to the Lord in terms of a wife who turns her back on her faithful husband. The imagery is taken from Hosea's personal experience which is like God's relationship to Israel.

1. Name four sins that Israel will be punished for.

2. What do you think would be a fair punishment for someone who betrayed you?

Day 6. God's Love for Israel. Hosea 11.

1. Tell two things that God did for Israel out of love.

2. Share a time when someone you loved hurt your feelings.

How did you react? (Did you seek revenge or offer forgiveness?)

Week 28

Key Memory Verse: "And what does the LORD require of you? To act justly and to love mercy and to walk humbly with your God" (Micah 6:8).

Day 1. A Locust Plague. Joel 2:1-13, 25-27.

Joel shows how God passed judgment on his people with a locust plague which tore up the country.

1. What did the locusts do to the land?

2. How do you respond to disaster?

Name someone who you know you could count on in an emergency.

Day 2. God's Majestic Anger. Amos 4.

Amos focuses on a materialistic nation that produces great injustice. Amos believes and preaches that religion involves doing justice.

1. Name at least two things that show the Israelites had grown mainly interested in their own luxury and pleasure.

2. Discuss the meaning of *injustice.*

Think about some of the injustices in the world today that make you angry. What can you do to change these injustices?

Day 3. A Blood Feud. Obadiah 1:1-15.

Obadiah, the shortest book in the Old Testament, warns Edom of the coming judgment of God as a result of their hostile actions toward Israel.

1. Why was Edom being punished?

2. Tell about a time when you have been treated badly by a close relative.

Day 4. Jonah goes to Nineveh. Jonah 3.
Jonah calls Israel to repentance and reminds her of her mission to preach God's mercy and forgiveness to all the nations.
1. Why did God decide not to destroy Nineveh?
2. Saying you're sorry for a wrong thing you've done is sometimes not enough. Share other ways you can show you are sorry.

Day 5. Jonah's Anger. Jonah 4.
1. Why was Jonah angry at the Lord's compassion for the people of Nineveh?
2. Imagine that someone at school or work has treated you unfairly for five years. At last this person's mean acts are seen by the principal or supervisor. You are relieved as this bully is taken to the office. However, when they come out of the office, they smile and shake hands. You are told the bully has confessed, apologized and promises never to act this way again. How would you feel about this outcome?

Day 6. What God Wants Us to Be. Micah 6.
(Preschool: Micah 6:1-8)
Micah exposes corruption in every level of the ancient Hebrew society but closes with a promise of forgiveness and restoration.
1. What does God require of you?
2. Describe ways you can walk humbly with God.

Week 29

Key Memory Verse: "Administer true justice; show mercy and compassion to one another. Do not oppress the widow or the fatherless, the alien or the poor. In your hearts do not think evil of each other" (Zechariah 7:9-10).

Day 1. God's Anger Against Nineveh. Nahum 1.

(Preschool: Nahum 1:1-8)

Nahum focuses on God's judgment on Nineveh for her wickedness. The book ends with the destruction of Nineveh. The Nineveh of this passage is the same Nineveh that repented and was saved from God's judgment in Jonah's time.

1. How does this passage show that God is fair in his judgment?

2. Nineveh broke its promise to change. Share a time when you broke a promise.

What were the consequences?

Day 2. Habakkuk and God. Habakkuk 1.

Habakkuk addresses God, not people, and confronts honestly a question plaguing the Israelites, "Why do bad things happen to good people?"

1. What thing did God do that he said the Israelites would not believe even if they were told?

2. Discipline at work, home or school may at times seem harsh or unjust even though it may be in your best interest. Share a time when this has happened to you.

Day 3. The Future of Jerusalem. Zephaniah 3.

(Preschool: Zephaniah 3:12-17)

Zephaniah condemns the corrupt and impure religious practices of the Israelite nation. The book describes the destruction of the wicked and the restoration of the faithful.

1. What will God do to the people of Jerusalem after the city is destroyed?

2. How can you rely on verse 17 when life is hard?

Day 4. Changing Directions. Haggai 1.

Haggai chronicles the reconstruction of the temple in Jerusalem by those returning from captivity in Babylon. At the heart of Haggai's encouragement to rebuild the temple is the message to put God first.

1. What were the Israelites doing with their time and money? What did God want them to do?

2. What do your material things mean to you? (Are you satisfied with what you have? Do you find yourself always wanting more?)

Day 5. The Lord Blesses Jerusalem. Zechariah 8.

(Preschool: Zechariah 8:1-8, 14-17)

Zechariah, a contemporary with Haggai, shares his urgent zeal for the rebuilding of the temple. This priest/prophet concerns himself with the messianic hope and gives specific predictions about the coming of the Messiah.

1. What are the things God wants all people to do?

2. Verse 16 says, "Speak truth to one another." Share an experience when someone did not speak the truth to you.

How did this affect your relationship with that person?

Day 6. Promises and Expectations. Malachi 3:6-17.

Malachi tries to stir up a nation that had grown indifferent to God. He attempts to return to a living faith people who are simply "going through the motions."

1. How did God say the Israelites were robbing him?

2. Often we do not give God the opportunity to care for us and meet our needs. Share an experience when you had to depend totally on God because you knew you could not help yourself.

Part 5
The Gospels

Matthew
Mark
Luke
John

Week 30

Key Memory Verse: "Come to me, all you who are weary and burdened, and I will give you rest" (Matthew 11:28).

Day 1. The Beatitudes. Matthew 5:1-12. *Matthew tells Jesus' life story from his family tree to his death on the cross and resurrection. This Gospel presents Jesus as the Messiah and King promised in the Old Testament. It emphasizes Jesus' authority in heaven and on earth.*

In this study we begin reading the Sermon on the Mount which is contained in chapters 5—7. In the Sermon Jesus gives the basic standards for living out the Christian life.

1. Who does Jesus call blessed in these verses?

2. Name something about yourself that Jesus might call blessed.

Day 2. Let Your Light Shine. Matthew 5:13-16.

1. Why did Jesus tell the people to let their light shine before others?

2. How can you "let your light shine before others"?

Day 3. Love Your Enemies. Matthew 5:38-48.

1. What does Jesus tell us to do in order that we may be children of our Father in heaven?

2. Who is your enemy? Tell about someone you're angry with or who you don't like.

It is hard to love our enemies. We cannot do this alone. Ask

God to help you change your heart. Pray that God can work on your enemy's heart as well.

Day 4. Learning to Pray. Matthew 6:5-18.
1. How does Jesus say we should pray?
2. When do you pray?
   Tell about a special place where you usually pray.

Day 5. Serving Two Masters. Matthew 6:19-24.
1. Name the two masters Jesus says we cannot serve at the same time. Why can't we serve both simultaneously?
2. What happens when you try to do two things at once? (For instance, have you ever had two tests or two office projects due on the same day? Have you ever tried to study, write a report, or read a book while watching television or visiting on the phone? How do you feel when Mom or Dad wants you to get dressed quickly and you are watching your favorite cartoon or looking at your favorite book?)

Day 6. Wise and Foolish Builders. Matthew 7:24-29.
1. What is the difference between the wise person and the foolish person?
2. Tell about a time when you tried to build or do something that didn't work out.
   How would you do it differently next time?

Special Activity: The Lord's Prayer
Memorize a verse of the Lord's Prayer each day for five days and practice saying all of it on the sixth day.

Week 31

Key Memory Verse: "Love the LORD *your God with all your heart and with all your soul and with all your mind" (Matthew 22:37).*

Day 1. The Sower. Matthew 13:1-23.
1. What is the point Jesus is trying to make in this parable?
2. What kind of soil describes you?

Day 2. Parable of the Weeds. Matthew 13:24-43.
1. How did Jesus explain "The Parable of the Weeds"?
2. Why is it sometimes difficult for families to see one another as especially talented individuals?

If you and your family members were strangers but met briefly at school or work, what one thing would you say you really liked about each one?

Day 3. Jesus Walks on Water. Matthew 14:22-36.
1. Why did Jesus walk on the water?
2. How do you keep yourself focused on God?

Day 4. Kingdom of Heaven. Matthew 19:16-30.
1. What does Jesus tell the young man he must do in order to receive eternal life?
2. In what ways do our possessions get in the way of our relationship with God?

Day 5. The Workers. Matthew 20:1-16.

1. How much did the vinekeeper promise all the workers?

2. Pretend that on Monday you were promised a great reward for doing good work at home, school or your job during the week. A family member, fellow student, or a worker received the same promise on Friday of that week. On Sunday you both received the same reward. Is this fair? Why or why not?

Day 6. Jesus Betrayed. Matthew 26:1-5, 14-16.

1. Who betrayed Jesus and what did he receive for doing this?

2. Tell about a time someone you trusted hurt you with his or her words or actions. Tell about a time that you hurt someone who trusted you.

Week 32

Key Memory Verse: "And surely I am with you always, to the very end of the age" (Matthew 28:20).

Day 1. Jesus Prepares. Matthew 26:17-46.
(Preschool: Matthew 26:26-29, 36-46)
1. Jesus knows that soon he will be betrayed and arrested. What two things did Jesus do before his arrest?
2. The night before Jesus was arrested was a very lonely, agonizing time. Describe how it feels to be lonely.

Day 2. Jesus Arrested. Matthew 26:47-68.
1. Why didn't Jesus call on the angels to help him?
2. If you were in danger, what ways would you use to defend yourself?

Day 3. Jesus before Pilate. Matthew 27:11-26.
1. Identify the six questions Pilate asked Jesus, the chief priests and the crowd.
2. If you heard what you thought were false rumors or lies about a friend or family member, what questions would you ask if you were trying to find out the truth?

Day 4. Crucifixion of Jesus. Matthew 27:27-44.
1. Name five things the soldiers did to Christ before the crucifixion.

2. Jesus suffered a great deal of physical pain and humiliation, and yet remained steadfast. What things in your life would help you to be strong if you were in a situation like this?

Day 5. Death of Jesus. Matthew 27:45-66.
1. What were some of the events that took place the moment Jesus died?
2. If you have known someone who died, what changes took place in your life as a result of his or her death?

Day 6. Resurrection of Jesus. Matthew 28.
1. What did the angel tell Mary Magdalene and the other Mary?
2. What is the best news you have ever received?
   What effect did this news have on you?

Week 33

Key Memory Verse: "The kingdom of God is near. Repent and believe the good news!" (Mark 1:15).

Day 1. Baptism of Jesus. Mark 1:1-20.

Mark is commonly thought to have been the first Gospel written in the New Testament. This Gospel presents Jesus as the Son of God. It was probably written for people who knew little about the Christian faith.

1. What happened when Jesus was baptized?

2. In verse 17 Jesus says, "Follow me and I will make you fishers of men." How can you relate this to your life today?

Day 2. Jesus Heals Many. Mark 1:21-32.

1. Why do you think Jesus spent time healing the sick and crippled?

2. If you had healing powers like Jesus, who would you heal? Why?

Day 3. Jesus Heals a Paralytic. Mark 2:1-12.

1. How did Jesus show the people that the Son of man had authority upon the earth?

2. Share about something in your life which you have authority over.

   What or who gives you this authority?

Day 4. Calling of Levi. Mark 2:13-17.

1. Why was Jesus eating with the tax collectors and sinners?

2. What type of people do you spend time with?

In what ways do you think you influence them and in what ways do they influence you?

Day 5. The Twelve Disciples. Mark 3:13-19.

1. What did Jesus appoint the disciples to do?

2. Try to name twelve people who mean a great deal to you.

Day 6. Teachers of the Law. Mark 3:20-35.

1. What were the teachers of the Law who came down from Jerusalem thinking about Jesus?

How did Jesus answer them?

2. Jesus' teaching shows that we can do much more if we work together. Describe a time when you were not strong enough to lift or move an object, but with the help of others you moved it easily.

Special Activity: The Twelve Disciples

How many of the twelve disciples' names can you say from memory? Try to learn them all.

Week 34

Key Memory Verse: "Don't be afraid; just believe" (Mark 5:36).

Day 1. Jesus Calms the Storm. Mark 4:35-41.

1. Why were the disciples so terrified during the storm?

2. The power of nature is awesome. Imagine the most destructive acts of nature—volcanos, hurricanes and tornados. Now imagine having the power to stop this destruction in an instant by saying a word. What do you think the reaction of those around you would be?

What would your reaction be if you were a witness to such a miracle?

Day 2. A Legion of Demons. Mark 5:1-20.

1. Why was Legion afraid of Jesus?

What did Jesus do to help this man?

2. Jesus asked for the name of this man's demon. Name what you fear the most and ask Jesus to help you confront that fear.

Day 3. Miracles of Healing. Mark 5:21-43.

1. How was the woman in the crowd healed?

2. If you found yourself in a crowd with Jesus and believed that if you reached out and touched him your life would be transformed forever, what changes would you pray for?

Day 4. John the Baptist Beheaded. Mark 6:14-29.

1. Why had King Herod ordered John the Baptist killed?

2. What kind of power do you think Jesus gives us today? How can you use this power?

Day 5. Jesus Feeds Five Thousand. Mark 6:30-44.

1. Why do you think Jesus wanted to retreat to a quiet place? What happened when he left?

2. Think of a time when you were with a lot of people. (Perhaps you were celebrating a holiday or sightseeing.) How did you feel at the end of the day?

Day 6. The Pharisees. Mark 7:1-23.

1. What did Jesus tell the Pharisees after they complained about his disciples being "unclean"?

What did he tell the crowd?

2. Share a time when you said something or did something you wish you could take back.

Week 35

Key Memory Verse: "Everything is possible for him who believes" (Mark 9:23).

Day 1. Healing. Mark 7:24-37.

1. How did the people react to all the healing they had seen Jesus do?

2. What is your reaction to Jesus after reading about the miracles he performed?

Day 2. Jesus Feeds Many. Mark 8:1-21.

1. Why were the disciples worried about having enough bread to eat?

2. How can you help those who are physically hungry?
How can you help those who are spiritually hungry?

Day 3. Jesus and Peter. Mark 8:22-38.

1. Who did people think Jesus was?
Who did Peter think he was?

2. Peter was with Jesus for a long time before he fully understood who he was. Do you know who Jesus is? Share this.

Day 4. The Transfiguration. Mark 9:1-13.

1. Tell about Jesus' Transfiguration.

2. What religious person do you admire the most?
Is it wrong to admire and respect someone whom you consider holy?

Day 5. The Disciples. Mark 9:33-41.

1. On the road to Capernaum what were the disciples arguing about?

2. Power and responsibility go hand in hand. If you are a gardener and want to grow a crop of tomatoes, what must you do?

If you are in charge of other people and expect them to work very hard, what must you do?

Day 6. Little Children. Mark 10:13-31.

1. What did Jesus tell his disciples about children?

2. In what ways are we all to be like children?

Week 36

Key Memory Verse: "Love your neighbor as yourself" (Mark 12:31).

Day 1. Blind Bartimaeus. Mark 10:46-52.

1. How did Bartimaeus receive his sight?

2. If you were blind, what would you miss seeing the most? Close your eyes and describe it in detail.

Day 2. Triumphal Entry. Mark 11:1-11.

1. Describe Jesus' entrance into Jerusalem.

2. Tell about the biggest parade you've seen.

Day 3. The Fig Tree. Mark 11:20-33.

1. What did Jesus say about prayer?

2. Think of one person you are angry with. Ask God to help you forgive that person and pray for him or her.

Day 4. Paying Taxes. Mark 12:13-17.

1. How did Jesus answer the Pharisees about paying taxes?

2. What belongs to God?

Day 5. The Greatest Commandments. Mark 12:28-44.

1. In your own words tell what the greatest and second greatest commandments are.

2. Read verse 44 again. What sacrificial gift can you give to God?

Day 6. Signs of the End. Mark 13:1-31.
(Preschool: Mark 13:3-4, 10-11)
1. Why did Jesus tell the disciples not to worry about what to say if they were arrested and brought to trial?
2. God's Holy Spirit can help you express your feelings even at the most difficult moments. Share a time when you were surprised by your own words.

Special Activity: The Greatest Commandments
Memorize the greatest and second-greatest commandments from Mark 12:29-31.

Week 37

Key Memory Verse: "Go into all the world and preach the good news to all creation" (Mark 16:15).

Day 1. Jesus Is Anointed. Mark 14:1-11.

1. Why was Jesus so pleased that the woman used her expensive perfume to anoint him?

2. How can you show Jesus that you love him?

Day 2. Jesus Predicts Peter's Denial. Mark 14:27-31.

1. What did Jesus tell Peter that the disciple would do before daybreak?

2. Share a time when you failed someone. How did this feel?

Day 3. Peter's Denial. Mark 14:66-72.

1. How did Peter respond when he was questioned in the courtyard?

2. Guilt is feeling bad about something you did wrong. Shame is feeling bad because you see yourself as bad or rotten. Did Peter feel guilt or shame?

Have you ever felt guilty or ashamed? Describe these feelings if you can.

Day 4. Pilate's Questions. Mark 15:1-20.

1. What question did Pilate ask Jesus?
How did he answer?

How did Jesus answer the accusations of the chief priests?

2. It is very difficult to be silent when others are telling lies about you. Why do you think Jesus did not defend himself with words? What would your reaction be if someone was telling lies about you?

Day 5. Mocking Jesus. Mark 15:16-32.

1. Why did the chief priests mock Jesus and ask him why he didn't save himself?

2. It is easy to make fun of someone when you are in a crowd and can escape retaliation. Have you ever joined others in being cruel to someone? Explain what happened.

How did you feel later when you were alone?

Day 6. The Resurrection. Mark 16:1-8.

1. What happened when the women arrived at the tomb?

2. Describe one of the happiest days of your life, and tell why you were so happy.

Week 38

Key Memory Verse: "Glory to God in the highest, and on earth peace to men on whom his favor rests" (Luke 2:14).

Day 1. Birth of John the Baptist Foretold. Luke 1:1-25.

(Preschool: Luke 1:5-25)

Luke gives us a joy-filled account of the life of Jesus from his birth. This book was probably originally part of a larger body of work including Acts.

1. Pick out three pieces of information the angel of the Lord gave to Zechariah.

Zechariah and Elizabeth faithfully waited many years for God to answer their prayer. What have you been praying about for a long time?

Day 2. Birth of Jesus Foretold. Luke 1:26-56.

(Preschool: Luke 1:26-45)

1. How does the angel Gabriel describe the child that will be born to Mary?

2. Describe your most outstanding characteristic—that part of you which you feel makes you special or unique.

Day 3. Birth of John the Baptist. Luke 1:57-80.

(Preschool: Luke 1:57-66)

1. What greatly amazed the neighbors of Zechariah after his son was born?

2. Do you know the story behind your name? (Were you named after a relative, friend or famous person?)

What is your favorite name and why?

Day 4. Birth of Jesus. Luke 2:1-20.

1. What did the angel of the Lord tell the shepherds?

How do we celebrate the birth of Jesus today?

2. What family tradition reminds you to think about Jesus during Christmas?

Day 5. Jesus' Childhood. Luke 2:21-52.

1. Jesus is at the temple twice in these verses. In what ways are his two visits different from one another?

2. Jesus asked these teachers many questions about God. What questions about God would you have if you were with a group of religious teachers?

Day 6. Jesus Sends out Seventy-Two. Luke 10:1-24.

1. What did Jesus tell the appointed seventy-two people to say to others when they were welcomed?

2. These seventy-two people were given a job to do for God. Do you think God has given you a job to do? Explain.

Week 39

Key Memory Verse: "Blessed rather are those who hear the word of God and obey it" (Luke 11:28).

Day 1. The Good Samaritan. Luke 10:25-37.

1. What did Jesus tell an expert in the Law he must do to inherit eternal life?

2. Use the glossary to look up the word *mercy* and discuss its meaning.

To understand "neighbor," think of a time when you showed mercy to another. How is our church a neighbor?

Our country?

Day 2. Six Woes. Luke 11:37-53.

1. How did the Pharisees and the teachers of the Law feel about Jesus after this discussion?

2. Reread verse 46. Sometimes it is difficult to be a Christian in our world today. Describe different ways you can help others understand the love of God.

Day 3. Do Not Worry. Luke 12:22-34.

1. Why did Jesus tell his disciples not to worry about clothes and food?

Was he telling them not to work for their living?

2. What things cause you to worry most? (Speaking these things aloud to others may be the first step in helping you with this worry.)

Day 4. Crippled Woman Healed. Luke 13:10-17.

1. Why was the synagogue ruler upset?

2. Why does Jesus call the synagogue ruler a hypocrite?

What things do you do that might appear opposite of what you "say" you ought to do?

Day 5. The Lost Sheep. Luke 15:1-10.

1. What did Jesus tell the tax collectors and "sinners" would cause a great rejoicing in heaven?

2. Use the glossary and look up the words *righteous* and *repent.* Discuss the different attitudes that accompany these definitions.

Why would there be more celebration for one over the other?

Day 6. Parable of the Lost Son. Luke 15:11-32.

1. Why was the lost son treated so well by his father when he returned home?

What words would you use to describe this father?

2. If there is someone in your life that you feel has wronged you, stop now and pray for a forgiving spirit.

Special Activity: Answers to Prayer

In week six you began a prayer journal. Take time to look over your prayer entries. Can you see how God is working or has worked to answer one or more of your prayers?

Week 40

Key Memory Verse: "Let the little children come to me, and do not hinder them, for the kingdom of God belongs to such as these" (Luke 18:16).

Day 1. The Shrewd Manager. Luke 16:1-15.

1. What did Jesus say about trust and dishonesty?

2. Name three things which God has given you or your family. (These may be material things, spiritual gifts or personal attributes.)

In what ways do you care for these things?

Day 2. The Rich Man and Lazarus. Luke 16:19-31.

1. What reason did Abraham give the rich man for not sending Lazarus back to save the five brothers?

2. If you were to share your knowledge and understanding of God with five people, who would they be and why?

Day 3. The Persistent Widow. Luke 18:1-8.

1. How did Jesus tell the disciples that people can receive justice?

2. When something is unjust it means it is unfair. Share a time in your life when you felt you were treated unjustly.

Share a time when you may have treated someone else unjustly.

Day 4. The Teachings of Jesus. Luke 18:9-30.

1. What do you think the tax collector in verse 13 and those Jesus speaks of in verse 17 have in common?

2. The rich ruler in verse 18 was put to the test by Jesus as to what he was truly committed to. What things are you truly committed to?

What would be the most difficult thing for you to give up?

Day 5. Resurrection of Jesus. Luke 24:1-35.

1. What took place before the two men going to Emmaus recognized Christ?

2. How do you begin to recognize Christ in those around you?

Day 6. Jesus Appears. Luke 24:36-53.

1. What had been written in the Law of Moses, the Prophets and the Psalms that Jesus says has now been fulfilled?

2. Jesus felt the disciples needed physical proof that it was indeed he who had returned. In what ways does God provide you with physical proof of his love and care?

Week 41

Key Memory Verse: "In the beginning was the Word, and the Word was with God, and the Word was God" (John 1:1).

Day 1. Jesus Teaches Nicodemus. John 3:1-21.

John appears to have been written with a Christian audience in mind. Rather than focusing on historical events of Jesus' ministry, John uses a different, more reflective, style to present Jesus as the Son of God.

1. Why did Nicodemus believe that Jesus was able to perform miracles?

2. Nicodemus was a religious leader and yet he found this teaching of Jesus difficult to understand. What teaching concerning God do you find hardest to understand?

Day 2. Testimony about Jesus. John 3:22-36.

1. What did John say the "one whom God has sent" does?

2. If you were asked to speak for God, what would you choose to say?

Day 3. The Woman at the Well. John 4:1-26.

1. What does Jesus mean when he talks about living water in verses 10-14?

Why does Jesus ask the woman about her husband?

2. How can you be a friend to someone in your school, at work or at church who is different?

Day 4. The Good Shepherd. John 10:1-30.

(Preschool: John 10:11-18)

1. Name three things the good shepherd does for his flock.

2. Discuss different ways you would try to help if you thought a friend or family members might be in trouble.

Day 5. The Death of Lazarus. John 11:1-44.

1. Why did Jesus wait so long to go to his friend Lazarus?

2. Share an experience you have had with the death of a friend or family member.

Mary, Martha and Jesus felt very sad. Maybe you have felt this way also. Remember that the promise Jesus makes in verse 25 to those Lazarus left behind is your promise as well.

Day 6. Jesus Washes His Disciples' Feet. John 13:1-17.

1. What is the new command Jesus gives his disciples?

2. Jesus asks us to love others as he has loved us. Think about one person you feel angry with or dislike. Share your feelings about that person, and then pray that God will help you love that person.

Week 42

Key Memory Verse: "Do not let your hearts be troubled. Trust in God; trust also in me" (John 14:1).

Day 1. Promise of the Holy Spirit. John 14:15-31.

1. Identify at least two different titles Jesus used for the Holy Spirit.

2. When you find yourself in an unfamiliar or strange situation, what things bring you comfort and help you feel less afraid?

Day 2. Vine and Branches. John 15:1-17.

1. What is Jesus talking about when he describes the vine and the branches?

2. How does God prune our branches?

Day 3. Grief Turns to Joy. John 16:17-33.

1. Why does Jesus say in verse 26, "I'm not saying that I will ask the Father on your behalf"?

2. Share an experience in your life when you saw good things come out of a bad situation.

Day 4. The Crucifixion. John 19:14-42.

(Preschool: John 19:14-30, 38-42)

1. Who stayed with Jesus as he died on the cross?

2. Even as he was dying, Jesus made sure his mother would be taken care of. Is there anyone that comes to your mind that needs your help or depends on you for care (physical or emotional)?

What are some ways you can go about providing that care?

Day 5. Jesus Appears to Thomas. John 20:1-23.

1. What made Thomas believe that Jesus was truly alive?

2. Sometimes it is hard to recognize Jesus even when we are looking directly at him. One way which we are able to see Christ is through the actions of others. Share an experience when someone acted on behalf of Christ with you (by helping you or praying for you) and you did not recognize Christ in them.

Others are also able to see Christ through our actions toward them. Can you think of a situation recently when others were able to recognize Christ in you?

Day 6. Feed My Sheep. John 21:1-25.

1. What are the three things Jesus asked Peter to do for him?

What question did Jesus pose to Peter before asking him to do each thing?

2. Peter is asked to care for others out of his love for Christ. Think of one person whom you find "unlovable." How can you reach out to this person through your love for Christ?

Part 6
Church History

Acts

Week 43

Key Memory Verse: "They devoted themselves to the apostles' teaching and to the fellowship, to the breaking of bread and to prayer" (Acts 2:42).

Day 1. Jesus Taken Up into Heaven. Acts 1:1-11.

Acts continues the narrative of Luke as it follows Christianity from the resurrection of Jesus to the establishment of the church. This book includes an account of the missionary journeys of Paul and concludes with him preaching unhindered in Rome.

1. What command did Jesus give his disciples?

2. Share the last time you were promised something very exciting and wonderful, perhaps a gift or a vacation.

Describe your feelings as you waited to receive the gift.

Day 2. A New Apostle. Acts 1:12-26.

1. How did the eleven disciples choose a new apostle?

2. Describe a difficult decision you have had to make.

How did you go about making your decision?

Day 3. The Holy Spirit. Acts 2:1-13.

1. When did the Holy Spirit come to the disciples?

Tell three things that occurred when the Holy Spirit came.

2. If you wanted to communicate the love of God to someone who did not speak your language, how would you go about doing so?

Day 4. Peter Speaks to the Crowd. Acts 2:14-47.
(Preschool: Acts 2:14, 36-47)

1. What three things did the believers devote themselves to after the three thousand people were baptized?

2. Can you name at least five things that we do regularly to celebrate our worship time on Sundays?

Day 5. The Crippled Beggar. Acts 3:1-16.

1. What did the crippled man expect to get from Peter and John?

2. There are many people with different needs in our world. List several ways you might help a person in need.

Day 6. Apostles Persecuted. Acts 5:12-42.

1. How did Gamaliel save the apostles?

2. Share an experience when you felt so strongly about something that you had to speak out even though it may not have been popular to do so and you risked being made fun of.

The disciples chose seven men known to be full of the Spirit and wisdom to administer the daily distribution of food. Among these men was Stephen, who became the church's first martyr.

Week 44

Key Memory Verse: "He has shown kindness by giving you rain from heaven and crops in their seasons; he provides you with plenty of food and fills your heart with joy" (Acts 14:17).

Day 1. Saul's Conversion. Acts 8:1-3; 9:1-19.

1. What did the Lord tell Ananias about Saul?

2. Ananias was afraid to do what God asked him to do. Have you ever felt afraid to do something which you knew God would have you do? Share the experience.

Day 2. Saul Preaches. Acts 9:19-31.

1. Why were people surprised to hear Saul preaching about Jesus?

2. What changes would you like to make in your life? How might others react to these changes?

Day 3. Peter's Vision. Acts 10:1-23.

1. Why didn't Peter want to eat the food God told him to eat in his vision?

2. Peter's Jewish heritage was very important to him. What is your religious heritage?

Has this heritage helped you better understand your relationship to God? Why or why not?

Day 4. Cornelius' House. Acts 10:24-48.

1. What very important message does Peter realize in verses 34-35?

2. God cannot be defined; he is the ultimate mystery. When was the last time you were "surprised" by God?

Day 5. Paul and Silas in Prison. Acts 16:16-40.

Saul, who is given the new name Paul, *sets off on his first missionary journey accompanied by Barnabas. After an argument about John Mark, Paul and Barnabas separate. Then, Paul takes Silas on his second missionary journey, while Barnabas and Mark sail for Cyprus.*

1. Why were Paul and Silas thrown into prison?

2. Paul and Silas showed kindness to the jailer. Think of someone in your life that you feel has been unkind or unfair to you. Pray now for that person and for your own attitude toward him or her.

Day 6. Paul in Corinth. Acts 18:1-17.

1. How did the Jews in Corinth treat Paul?

2. Paul was afraid, but the Lord comforted him in a vision. How does God comfort you when you are afraid?

How does God use you to comfort others?

Special Activity: Spiritual Journey

Using your prayer journal, record each family member's spiritual journey. Date this record and continue to add to it.

Week 45

Key Memory Verse: "You will be his witness to all men of what you have seen and heard. And now what are you waiting for? Get up, be baptized and wash your sins away, calling on his name (Acts 22:15-16).

Day 1. Paul in Jerusalem. Acts 22:30—23:35.

(Preschool: Acts 22:30; 23:12-35)

1. Why did the Pharisees and Sadducees begin to argue?

2. Share an experience when you feel you may have been falsely accused of doing or saying something.

What were some of your feelings when this happened?

Day 2. Paul Testifies. Acts 26:1-32.

1. What reason does Paul say that the Jews had for wanting to kill him?

2. Paul recounts his personal spiritual journey. Share your journey to date and, most specifically, your earliest memories of an awareness of God.

Day 3. Paul Sails for Rome. Acts 27:1-26.

1. Tell the warning and the encouragement Paul gave to the men on the ship.

2. Sometimes we encounter storms in our lives. Share something in your life now that seems to bring out any feelings of dread, fear or uncertainty.

Pray for God's presence in each of these situations.

Day 4. Shipwreck. Acts 27:27-44.

1. How did Paul help these men?

2. Daily pressures can take a toll on us physically and emotionally. What is the most stressful time of day for you?

What small changes could your family make to eliminate some of the daily stress you all encounter?

Day 5. Ashore on Malta. Acts 28:1-16.

1. Why did the people on Malta think Paul was a god?

2. Paul experienced the gift of hospitality at Malta, and he returned it with his own gifts. Look up the word *hospitable* in the glossary. What are some practical ways you can develop this gift?

Day 6. Paul Preaches under Guard. Acts 28:17-31.

1. Who was Paul preaching to?

Who did he tell them that God's salvation had been sent to?

2. Paul arrived in Rome and saw the Lord keep his promise to him. What are the most recent promises you have made?

How have you kept them?

Part 7
Letters

Romans
1 Corinthians
2 Corinthians
Galatians
Ephesians
Philippians
Colossians
1 Thessalonians
2 Thessalonians
1 Timothy
2 Timothy

Titus
Philemon
Hebrews
James
1 Peter
2 Peter
1 John
2 John
3 John
Jude
Revelation

Week 46

Key Memory Verse: "This righteousness from God comes through faith in Jesus Christ to all who believe. There is no difference, for all have sinned and fall short of the glory of God" (Romans 3:22-24).

Day 1. Paul Longs to Visit Rome. Romans 1:1-17.

Romans is a letter of instruction written by Paul, touching on the main truths of the gospel that he felt were needed in Rome. Written for a more sophisticated audience, this letter is the most profoundly theological of all Paul's letters. Paul discusses the nature of God's saving act in Christ and the new life which it has made available.

1. Why does Paul long to see the Christians in Rome?

2. Paul is writing a letter to people he cares about. Think of someone you would like to see. What things do you miss most about that person?

Day 2. Righteous Judgment. Romans 2:1-16.

1. What does *judgment* mean?

2. Tell about a time when you felt like someone was judging you.

Day 3. Righteousness through Faith. Romans 3:21-31.

Chapter three is seen as the central theological passage of the New Testament as it presents the core of the gospel message.

1. How do we sin against God?

How do we find righteousness?

2. Tell about a time that you did something bad to another person but that person forgave you for it.

Day 4. The Holy Spirit Intercedes. Romans 8:18-39.

1. How does the Holy Spirit help us in our weakness?

2. Paul says nothing can separate us from the love of God. Sometimes, however, we do feel distant from God. What things in your life do you feel separate you from God (for instance, worry, fears, hard times)?

Day 5. Living Sacrifices. Romans 12.

1. List seven gifts this passage speaks about. Give an example of each gift.

2. The love Paul speaks of in this chapter is not mere emotion, but is active love. Using this passage as your guide, discuss ways that your family can "actively" love one another as well as those around them.

Day 6. Submitting to Authorities. Romans 13:1-14.

1. What one rule sums up all the commandments?
   What is the fulfillment of the Law?

2. Describe the differences in the way you are treated by those who love you and those whom you feel do not love you.

Special Activity: Family Letter

Write a family letter to someone who is special to you. Be sure to include in your letter encouragement, information about yourself and questions about how the person is doing. Make it a point to pray for this person.

Week 47

Key Memory Verse: "Always give yourselves fully to the work of the Lord, because you know that your labor in the Lord is not in vain" (1 Corinthians 15:58).

Day 1. Divisions in the Church. 1 Corinthians 3:1-23.

In 1 Corinthians Paul gives practical advice to the church in Corinth on a series of problems. This book also gives us a unique opportunity to glance into the personal lives of first-century Christians.

1. What problems do you think had arisen in the Corinthian church?

2. What was the last quarrel you had with someone about? Has this been resolved?

Pray now for the person you have quarreled with.

Day 2. Idol Feasts. 1 Corinthians 10:14-22.

Some of the other problems facing the Corinthian church are lawsuits among believers, sexual immorality, food sacrificed to idols, and questions concerning marriage. In this passage Paul tells the Christians that they cannot be a part of both the Lord's Supper and feasts for idols.

1. Why is it wrong for the believers to eat food that was sacrificed to idols?

2. What does the Lord's Supper mean to you?

Day 3. Spiritual Gifts. 1 Corinthians 12:1-31.

(Preschool: 1 Corinthians 12:12-31)

1. Why have we each been given a spiritual gift?

2. Make a list of five qualities you like about yourself.

What kind of gift do these qualities indicate to you?

(Preschool parents: Have your children draw a picture of a human body naming as many parts as they can. Help them understand how important and interdependent each part is to the other. For example, our arms help our legs to balance our bodies when we walk.)

Day 4. Love. 1 Corinthians 13:1-13.

1. What three things remain when everything else has passed away?

What is the greatest?

2. Take time to hug each other warmly, and say "I love you."

Do one thing today that will put your words into action.

Day 5. Resurrection of the Dead. 1 Corinthians 15:35-44.

1. Our heavenly bodies are described as having a unique splendor. What about our earthly bodies?

2. There are many movies out today that present those who have died as evil and disgusting. Give an example of this kind of movie.

How does this compare with Paul's picture of our resurrected bodies?

Day 6. God's Comfort. 2 Corinthians 1:3-11.

Second Corinthians is Paul's follow-up letter to the church in Corinth. The most personal of all his letters expresses both joy and sadness as he relates to a difficult church congregation that he loves very much.

1. According to Paul, when does God comfort us?

2. Describe an experience you've had that helps you give com fort to others.

Week 48

Key Memory Verse: "I have been crucified with Christ and I no longer live, but Christ lives in me. The life I live in the body, I live by faith in the Son of God, who loved me and gave himself for me" (Galatians 2:20).

Day 1. Sowing Generously. 2 Corinthians 9:1-15.
(Preschool: 2 Corinthians 9:6-15)

1. How much should each person give?

2. Aside from giving money, what are some other ways you can give of yourself to others?

Day 2. Paul's Thorn. 2 Corinthians 12:1-21.

1. Paul's "thorn," or affliction, caused him to pray to the Lord to take it away. How did the Lord answer Paul's prayer?

2. What would you describe as your greatest weakness?

Begin praying today that in this weakness you will find God's strength.

Day 3. No Other Gospel. Galatians 1:1-24.

In Galatians Paul boldly confronts the problem of Jewish Christians who are telling the Gentile church at Galatia that circumcision and following the Mosaic Law are necessary for salvation.

1. How did Paul receive the gospel he preached?

2. Think about a time when you have been called a liar even though you were telling the truth. Describe the situation and how you felt.

Day 4. The Law and the Promise. Galatians 3:15-29.

1. How many years after God's covenant with Abraham was the Law introduced?

Why did God give people the Law?

2. Each instrument in an orchestra has its own unique shape and sound, yet when played by a master it blends with all the other unique sounds to become one musical voice. In the same way, we are all different, and yet in Christ we are one. Describe how we can become one with something or someone and remain unique.

Day 5. God's Love and Grace. Ephesians 3:1-21.

Ephesians manages to contain within its brief letter an encompassing view of the entire biblical message. In this book's development, the author suggests the privilege and destiny of believers as well as their duties.

1. In verses 16-19, what does the writer want his readers to understand about Christ?

2. Share with one another your understanding of Christ's love for you. (Does he love you? On what things do you base his love? How do you know?)

Day 6. Unity in the Body. Ephesians 4:1-16.

1. Why did God call some to be apostles, prophets, evangelists, pastors and teachers?

2. How would you go about finding out if something is true or false?

Week 49

Key Memory Verse: "Whatever happens, conduct yourselves in a manner worthy of the gospel of Christ" (Philippians 1:27).

Day 1. Armor of God. Ephesians 6:10-24.

1. Name the six pieces you would put on if you want the full armor of God. What is the sword of the Spirit?

2. Read verse 18 again. Discuss a country that is presently in a state of crisis (poverty, war, religious restrictions, prejudice). Pray now for the government and for those living in that country.

Day 2. Shine like Stars. Philippians 2:1-18.

Philippians, written by Paul while in prison, is one of his most affectionate letters. Addressed to the church at Philippi in Macedonia, it stresses that joy can be found in any situation.

1. How can we "shine like stars" for God?

2. What time of day is particularly difficult for your family to get through without complaining and arguing (for instance, dinner, bedtime, morning)? Discuss together ways each of you contribute to the chaos and how each can help.

Day 3. Christ Is Supreme. Colossians 3:1-17.

(Preschool: Colossians 3:12-17)

Colossians contains some of Paul's most eloquent writings about Jesus Christ. Paul writes this letter to correct the false teachings about Jesus that are being introduced to the newly founded church at Colossae.

1. What are we asked to clothe ourselves with?

2. Name someone whom you highly respect.

List five characteristics of that person which you feel are outstanding qualities. (These things are what this person has "clothed" himself or herself with.)

Day 4. Thessalonian Church. 1 Thessalonians 2:17—3:10.
First Thessalonians is our earliest record of the life of a Christian community and Paul's advice to them. Paul commends the church at Thessalonica for their dedication to Christ and to one another, and to encourage them.
1. Who did Paul send to help the Thessalonian church?
   How did he help?
2. Name someone in your life who makes a special effort to encourage and support you. How does that person encourage you?

Day 5. Living to Please God. 1 Thessalonians 4:1-18.
(Preschool: 1 Thessalonians 4:9-18)
This passage discusses "those who fall asleep." "Fallen asleep" is another way of saying that someone died. Because of Christ, we don't need to be afraid of death.
1. How can you live to please God?
2. If you could ask God one question about life after death, what would your question be?

Day 6. Stand Firm. 2 Thessalonians 2:13—3:15.
(Preschool: 2 Thessalonians 2:13—3:5)
Second Thessalonians records similar advice to that contained in the first letter but in a sterner approach.
1. What does Paul command the Thessalonians to do in verse 15?
2. What things about God do you believe are above debate?
   What are some things about God that you feel strongly about but still question?

Week 50

Key Memory Verse: "Now faith is being sure of what we hope for and certain of what we do not see" (Hebrews 11:1).

Day 1. False Teachers. 1 Timothy 1:1-11.

First Timothy provides guidance for church administration and opposes false teachings that were threatening the church.

1. What is the goal of the command against teaching false doctrines, as mentioned in verse 5?

2. Discuss some of the rules you have in your home. What is the "goal" for these rules.

Day 2. A Challenge to Timothy. 2 Timothy 2:1-26.

(Preschool: 2 Timothy 2:8-26)

Second Timothy is a heartfelt letter urging endurance as the main quality of a preacher of the gospel. Its farewell words provide a moving testimony of Christian stamina, long-suffering and hope in the face of certain martyrdom.

1. What was the false teaching being spread by Hymenaeus and Philetus?

2. Recall an instance when an untrue rumor was spread about you or a friend. How did this affect you?

Day 3. Doing What Is Good. Titus 3.

In the letter to Titus, Paul gives his friend practical advice on ways to help the difficult church in Crete.

1. According to verse 4, why did God save us?

2. How would you go about warning someone who was making trouble for you?

Day 4. Paul's Plea for Onesimus. Philemon 1:1-21.

Philemon is Paul's letter urging the owner of the runaway slave Ones-imus to forgive and accept him. Onesimus had become a Christian and and knew he needed to return to his master, but was afraid. While Paul does not attack slavery itself, he does affirm the teachings of Jesus on the value of every human soul and the church as a family of believers.

1. What kind of relationship did Paul ask Philemon to have with Onesimus?

2. Share an experience when you had to act as a "peacemaker" between two people or groups.

What can we do as a country to keep peace in the world?

Day 5. Jesus Made Like Us. Hebrews 2:5-18.

Hebrews addresses an audience of Jewish Christians who were on the point of giving up their Christian faith and returning to their Jewish beliefs and practices. This book insists there are reasons to choose Christ, urges people toward a new experience with God through Christ, and interprets the Old Testament, explaining many Jewish practices as symbols that prepare the way for Christ.

1. Why was it important for God to make Jesus like humanity?

2. According to verse 18 because Jesus suffered he was able to help others who suffered. Recall an experience in your life that was painful physically or emotionally. Because of that, in what ways are you more able to help another person who is going through a similar painful experience?

Day 6. By Faith. Hebrews 11.

To help the Jewish Christians understand Christianity better, the au-thor emphasizes the superiority of Jesus Christ to the prophets, the angels, Moses, the Levitical priests, and animal sacrifices.

1. Why is it impossible to please God without faith?

2. With verse one in mind, describe two things:

(a) What things do you hope for?

(b) What things are you certain of that you cannot see? (For example, we do see the sun rise every morning but we have faith it will rise even the night before, even when it is dark with no sign of sunlight.)

Week 51

Key Memory Verse: "Finally, all of you, live in harmony with one another; be sympathetic, love as brothers, be compassionate and humble" (1 Peter 3:8).

Day 1. Discipline. Hebrews 12:1-13.

1. Why does God discipline us?

2. Imagine a home with no rules or discipline. List the positive and negative things about being in a home like this.

What conclusions about discipline can you draw from your list?

Day 2. Love and Hospitality. Hebrews 13:1-25.

1. According to verse 16, what kinds of sacrifices are pleasing to God?

2. Share an experience you have had when you gave up something you wanted so another person could have it. What were your reasons for doing this?

Day 3. Trials and Temptations. James 1:19-27.

James is a sermon in the form of a letter which emphasizes how Christians ought to live.

1. What is the difference between a "hearer" of the Word and a "doer"?

2. Would you describe yourself as a hearer or a doer? Why?

Day 4. A Living Hope. 1 Peter 1:1-12.

First Peter comforts and encourages Christians who are persecuted for their faith. This letter was originally written for those Christians in the northern part of Asia Minor who were experiencing violent opposition.

1. What is of greater worth than gold?

What three things result from this?

2. Verses 8-9 describe a relationship in faith. How would you describe your present relationship with God?

Day 5. Making Calling and Election Sure. 2 Peter 1:1-21.

(Preschool: 2 Peter 1:3-11)

Second Peter warns against the problems of false teachers arising inside the Christian community. This letter also serves to strengthen faith in the Second Coming of Christ.

1. Why is it important to add the qualities listed in verses 5-7 to your faith?

2. What are some different ways you might develop these qualities in your life? (For example, even by doing this Bible study today you have cultivated the quality of knowledge of your faith.)

Day 6. Children of God. 1 John 2:28—3:24.

(Preschool: 1 John 2:28—3:3; 3:18-24)

First John seeks to correct the false teaching of those who denied that God had really become human in Jesus and explains basic truths about the Christian life.

1. Why are we called children of God?

2. Describe various ways you might take action in your love for God and all creation as verse 18 directs.

Week 52

Key Memory Verse: Holy, holy, holy is the Lord God Almighty, who was, and is, and is to come" (Revelation 4:8).

Day 1. This Is Love. 2 John.

The shortest book in the Bible, 2 John contains only 13 verses. 2 John teaches about love and obedience. It also warns Christians against showing hospitality to false teachers.

1. What is love according to John?

2. Name one person who helps you feel loved. Describe the various ways this person shows love to you.

Day 2. Faithfulness to the Truth. 3 John.

Third John gives guidelines for sharing hospitality to true Christian teachers.

1. What is John's advice to his friend Gaius?

2. What advice would you give to a friend who was dealing with a troublemaker?

Day 3. A Call to Hold On. Jude 1:1-25.

(Preschool: Jude 1:20-25)

Jude gives a clear picture of the character and methods of false teachers. The author urges his readers to stand firm in their faith in Jesus Christ and concludes with a poetic and moving doxology.

1. How are the readers of this letter encouraged to build themselves up?

2. How can you as family members help to build one another up?

Day 4. Seven Lampstands. Revelation 1:1-19.
(Preschool: Revelation 1:9-19)

About sixty years after Jesus left the earth, Christian people were troubled and began to ask questions about him. Revelation addresses these questions and gives a unique picture of Christ. Even though it's a book full of mysteries, it tells of Christ's future triumph over evil and gives hope to its original readers as well as those today.

Revelation speaks lasting truths to every generation of readers with its crucial message of final hope. This book concentrates on prophecy, completing the story begun in Genesis that God is in charge of history and will ultimately triumph.

1. What did the one "like a son of man" say to John?

2. What would you like most about being alive "forever and ever"? What would you like least?

Day 5. The Throne in Heaven. Revelation 4:1-11.

1. What words did the four living creatures continuously recite?

2. Describe in your own words what you think you might see if you were to go to heaven as a visitor.

Day 6. The New Jerusalem. Revelation 21:1-27.
(Preschool: Revelation 21:1-4, 22-27)

1. Tell five things about the Holy City that you find exciting.

2. From Genesis to Revelation we see that God has consistently acted throughout history to re-establish a rightful relationship with humanity. Using verses 3-4, discuss the various ways God will seal this loving relationship.

Using *The Family Bible Companion* in Your Church

Why use *The Family Bible Companion* as a churchwide program?
The goal of the book is to aid in establishing a routine of study that is accessible to busy people. These studies can be utilized by families who desire to broaden their understanding of Scripture. The program is set up to be done in the home, normally requiring ten- to fifteen-minute blocks of time. *The Family Bible Companion* is an excellent follow-up for those families whose children have been presented with gift Bibles from the church.

How Do We Get Started?
First, present *The Family Bible Companion* materials to your education committee. Make sure this program will be supported by the committee and church staff. Then recruit a leader or leaders who have a sincere love for the Bible and a desire to see others grow in the knowledge and understanding of God's word. The leader will be responsible for organizing and implementing the reading program.

You may want to introduce the book to the rest of the congregation during Sunday-morning worship. A program that fosters regular Bible study is in keeping with the spirit of worship. This also allows the congregation to be affirmed by the support of the church staff.

How Do We Tell Them?
Begin your publicity with an article in your church newsletter. The Sunday *The Family Bible Companion* is presented from the pulpit, a registration insert could be included in your bulletin. A flyer with an attached registration sheet can be sent home with all Sunday-school students. This is an important way to reach many families churched and unchurched.

Use any source of communication (bulletins, information sheets, and so on) that is available to you and reaches your broadest constituency. Remember, word-of-mouth is always the most effective publicity.

How Do We Keep Track?
Have a centralized location (booth or table) where the registration forms can be turned in. Two Sundays are recommended for registration. A large banner or sign on or near your registration locale is helpful in directing people for registration turn-in/pick-up. Have a sample book available plus extra registration forms. The primary source of registrations will probably come from your bulletin insert and Sunday-school flyer.

Once registration is complete, you'll know how many copies to order from your local Christian bookstore. Get the books into the hands of those who signed up as soon as possible to keep the momentum high.

How Do We Follow-Up?
To help people stay on track, you might want to arrange a follow-up program to encourage families through the year. This could be done through phone-calling, church-wide progress charts or quarterly parents' meetings.

Glossary

Ark of the Covenant: the chest containing the two stone tablets inscribed with the Ten Commandments, kept in the holiest part of the ancient Jewish Tabernacle.

Assyria: the name of a country and the mighty empire that dominated the ancient biblical world from the 9th to the 7th century B.C.

Baal: the name of the chief male god of the Phoenicians.

Babylon: an ancient city-state in the plain of Shinar, derived from Akkadian *babilu,* "gate of God." The capital of Babylonia: noted for wealth, luxury and wickedness.

Blessing: an invoking of divine favor.

Canaanites: inhabitants of Canaan, the more ancient name of Palestine.

Circumcision: a Jewish religious rite consisting in cutting away the foreskin covering the head of the male organ.

Concubine: a secondary or inferior wife.

Confession: a general acknowledgement of sin, or a form expressing this used in public worship.

Covenant: a binding and solemn agreement to do or keep from doing a specified thing. The term applied to various transactions between God and humans; and people with people.

Crucifixion: a Roman form of execution in which the victim was nailed or bound to a wooden cross and left to die.

Descendant: a person who is an offspring, however remote, of a certain ancestor, family, group, etc.

Discern: to recognize; make out clearly; to perceive.

Disciple: a student or follower of any teacher or school of religion, art or learning. In the Bible it usually means "the followers of Jesus."

Exile: specifically, the removal of defeated Israelites by the Babylonians in 587 B.C.

Faith: unquestioning belief in God that does not require proof or evidence. Complete trust, confidence or reliance.

Gentile: a non-Jew. The original Greek term translated "Gentiles" means "nations."

Gospel: originally the message of good news that God had revealed himself as gracious in the event of Jesus Christ. The term later came to designate also the literary form in which the good news of Jesus' life, death and resurrection is narrated; for example, the Gospel according to Mark.

Grace: the unmerited love and favor of God toward humankind.

Heaven: the state or place of perfect union with God and so of eternal life and supreme happiness, attained by the elect after death.

Hebrew: any member of a group of Semitic peoples tracing descent from Abraham, Isaac and Jacob.

Holy: that which has to do with God or the divine power and majesty.

Holy Spirit: the third Person in the Trinity. The Spirit of God.

Hospitable: friendly, kind and considerate to guests.

Israel: the name conferred by the angel upon Jacob. The Jewish people as descendants of Jacob. Ancient land of the Hebrews at the SE end of the Mediterranean. Kingdom in the north part of this region, formed by the tribes of Israel that broke with Judah and Benjamin.

Jerusalem: the first city of Palestine. "The Holy City" for three great religions: Christianity, Judaism and Islam.

Jew: member of the tribe or kingdom of Judah. A person descended or regarded as having descended from the ancient Hebrews of biblical times.

Judah: fourth son of Jacob, whose mother was Leah. The tribe descended from him, the strongest of the twelve tribes of Israel.

Justification: the act or process by which God brings people into proper relationship with himself. In Paul the justification or righteousness of God is to be received by faith, not works.

Kingdom of God (or rule of God): God's lordship over humankind and the world. The kingdom is the center of Jesus' message in the Synoptic Gospels.

Law: in the New Testament generally the revelation of God through Moses to the people of Israel embodied in the cultic, ritual and moral commandments of the Old Testament.

Leprosy: a progressive infectious disease that attacks the skin, flesh, nerves, etc.; it is characterized by nodules, ulcers, white scaly scabs, deformities and the eventual loss of sensations.

Levite: any member of the tribe of Levi, chosen to assist the priests in the temple and carry the ark of the covenant.

Manna: food miraculously provided for the Israelites in the wilderness.

Martyr: any of those persons who chose to suffer and die rather than give up their faith or principles.

Mercy: a refraining from harming or punishing offenders, enemies, persons in one's power, etc.; kindness in excess of what may be expected or demanded by fairness; forebearance and compassion.

Messiah: from the Hebrew term meaning "anointed one." It was used of the Davidic king, whose restoration was expected in Jesus' day. Its Greek equivalent is the basic designation of Jesus in the New Testament. He was believed to be the expected Messiah of Israel.

Miracle: an extraordinary event, contrary to normal expectations, a manifestation of the activity of God.

Missionary: the sending out of persons by a religious organization to preach, teach and convert.

Parable: a brief story that makes its point by the unusual development or imagery of the narrative. The various details do not function as allegory but are significant for the story itself.

Pharisee: a member of the ancient Jewish sect that rigidly observed the written Law, but also insisted on the validity of the oral, or traditional, law.

Philistine: a member of a non-Semitic people who lived in Philistia and repeatedly warred with the Israelites.

Priest: a holy person authorized to perform ritual and cultic acts whereby humans and God are enabled to commune with each other.

Prophecy: divinely inspired sayings, or utterances, of a prophet.

Prophet: a person who speaks for God as though under divine guidance.

Purpose: something one intends to get or do; intention; aim. The object for which something exists or is done.

Reconciliation: being brought into harmony.

Redemption: literally "to buy" or "take back," particularly the act or process of God's taking back sinful or rebellious humanity by means of the event of Jesus Christ.

Repentance: feeling of sorrow, etc., especially for wrongdoing.

Resurrection: or rising from the dead; a central hope in the New Testament based on the early Christians' belief that Jesus was raised from the dead by God.

Righteous: acting in a just, upright manner. Primarily the quality of God (see justification). Doing what is right before God.

Sabbath: the seventh day of the week (Saturday), set aside by the fourth commandment for rest and worship and observed as such by Jews and some Christian sects.

Sacrifice: the act of offering something held valuable to the deity. By the act of sacrifice, communion with the divine is initiated, re-established or continued.

Sadducees: a religious group of the intertestamental period who represented the priestly aristocracy of Jewish life. In distinction from the Pharisees, they held only to the written Mosaic Law and did not believe in resurrection.

Salvation: the state of complete liberation from sin, brokenness, and estrangement between humanity and God. In general, the New Testament locates salvation in the future, although its inauguration is already effected in Christ.

Samaritan: native or inhabitant of Samaria.

Sin: generally any act, whether in thought or deed, that violates the law or will of God. In the New Testament particularly, it denotes the broken or estranged relationship between the human race and God.

Sojourn: to live somewhere temporarily, a brief stay.

Spiritual Gift: a special way of serving God that is given to every Christian by the Holy Spirit.

Synagogue: an assembling of Jews for worship and religious study.

Tabernacle: the portable sanctuary carried by the Jews in their wanderings from Egypt to Palestine.

Temple: a building for the worship of a divinity or divinities. Anything viewed as the dwelling place of God or a divinity.

Temptation: something that tries to persuade; induce or entice, especially to something immoral or against God.

Tribulation: great misery or distress, deep sorrow. Something that causes suffering or distress.

Unconditional: without conditions. Freely given without requiring anything in return.

Wise: having or showing good judgment. Prompted by wisdom, judicious, sound.

Word of God: frequently a designation for the Bible. In the New Testament, however, it is used in close connection with the event of Jesus.

About the Authors

Kathy Comina has taught third-grade Sunday school since 1984 at Solana Beach Presbyterian Church, Solana Beach, California. She received her Bachelor of Science degree in Elementary Education from Indiana University and has been a Basic Skills Instructor K-6th grade with San Diego City Schools since 1984. Kathy has been an active member of Bible Study Fellowship since 1983.

Janice Cook has worked in the field of educational ministries since 1974. She has been Director of Children's Ministries at Solana Beach Presbyterian Church since 1987. Janice received her Bachelor of Arts degree in Psychology, Bachelor's in Preaching and Master of Arts degree in Ministry from Pacific Christian College. In 1978 Janice was ordained a pastor in the Independent Christian Church. Since 1989 she has been enrolled at the School of Theology at Claremont in the Master of Divinity degree program.

*"The grace of the Lord Jesus
be with God's people.
Amen."*
(Revelation 22:21)